A SURVIVOR'S GUIDE TO HOME SCHOOLING

WHAT THEY'RE SAYING ABOUT *A SURVIVOR'S GUIDE:*
"Luanne Shackelford and Susan White are the Erma Bombecks of Home Schooling. We've needed a book like this for a long time. — Outrageously funny, full of true to life home school advice!"

> Gregg Harris, author of *The Christian Home School* and instructor for the Home Schooling Workshop

"Hilarious, upbeat, realistic guide to home schooling. A Survivor's Guide to Home Schooling is a great book for both the veteran home schooler and the timid beginner."

> Mary Pride, author of *The NEW Big Book of Home Learning, The Next Big Book of Home Learning* and *Schoolproof*

A Survivor's Guide to Home Schooling

*Luanne Shackelford
and
Susan White*

CROSSWAY BOOKS • WHEATON, ILLINOIS
A DIVISION OF GOOD NEWS PUBLISHERS

Linotronic® Typesetting by TRC Enterprises,
10871 Sunset Hills Plaza, St. Louis, Missouri 63127.

Cover illustration and design: Meredith Johnson

First printing, 1988

Printed in the United States of America.

Library of Congress Catalog Card Number 88-70691

ISBN 0-89107-503-8

99		98		97		96	
15	14	13	12	11

❤ To our husbands— Ed Shackelford and
Michael White:
    We appreciate your continuing support
and encouragement. Thank you for your
confidence that we can home school, and
your unselfishness while we do it.

❤ To our children— David, Nathan, Daniel,
Joy, Ariana, Peter and Luke Shackelford,
and Renada and Michaela White:
    We appreciate your love and obedience.
May you continue to grow like the Lord
Jesus, in wisdom and stature and favor
with God and man.

❤ To our parents— Robert and Barbara Seelye
and Chuck and Imogene Bailie:
    We appreciate all you have taught us by
instruction and example. Thank you for the
sacrifices you made to benefit us.

TABLE OF
Contents

Preface

You Absolutely Must Read This Preface!

I f you are the type of mother who is always on top of things, this book is not for you. If you answer "Yes" to seven or more of the following questions, reading this book will cause you to lose faith in womankind and embarrass the rest of us.

SURVEY

Yes No

☐ ☐ 1. Do you cook a hot breakfast every morning?

☐ ☐ 2. Is the laundry always folded and put away when you go to bed?

☐ ☐ 3. Do you bake bread more than once a month?

☐ ☐ 4. Do you iron (other than on Sunday morning)?

❑ ❑ 5. Do you sew more than ten garments a year?

❑ ❑ 6. Are your dishes done a half-hour after each meal?

❑ ❑ 7. Do you have your lesson plans ready a week in advance?

❑ ❑ 8. Do you bathe your children every night?

❑ ❑ 9. Do you have a filing system for your mail and other paperwork?

❑ ❑ 10. Do you plan your menus for the month?

❑ ❑ 11. Do you often get up before 5:45 A.M.?

❑ ❑ 12. Do you have a cottage industry?

❑ ❑ 13. Do you rarely raise your voice in frustration or anger?

If you passed this test, congratulations! Instead of buying this book, take yourself to lunch. You deserve it! We all admire you and hope you won't drop in unannounced.

The rest of you, turn the page . . .

Do Real People Do This?

"All the world is mad, but me and thee, and at times thou art a bit odd, methinks."
— Quaker proverb

As you begin to think about home teaching your children, you will in most cases feel good about the idea, frightened by the responsibility, and overwhelmed by the question of where to begin.

This is normal!

It *is* a big responsibility, and a sobering thought, that the buck stops with you when you take on home schooling. The first thing you usually do is go find a bunch of books on home schooling. Some authors paint a beautiful picture of patient mothers who never raise their voices, living in houses joyfully cleaned by children who rarely bicker and who are eager to learn their multiplication tables. I don't know anyone whose home is like that! Most of these books are written by men who assume the best about what goes on behind closed doors, bless their hearts!

This book is written by a real home schooling mom. I have seven children and I have been home teaching for five years. I enjoy the time I'm spending with my kids, and to me, it is worth all the hassle; but a hassle it is, nevertheless! I am a normal mother working at trying to keep my sanity, and my kids are normal kids who can drive me crazy! They spill their milk and leave toys lying around the house. They push each other around and yell, "*Mom!* Tell him to stop lookin' at me!" I have to *make* them do work around the house and *make* them eat like human beings. If I did not remind them, our pets would die of starvation and some of my kids would go to church barefoot without batting an eye. My big kids have taught the little ones to burp loudly and then bellow, "*Excuse Me!*" and to say, "Guess what, mom!" "What, sweetie?" "*That's what!*" (uproarious laughter). This keeps up until they are threatened with bodily harm unless they cool it.

They are wonderful! They are no more perfect than I am. I love them!

When you decide to home teach, nothing changes. You are the same mother and they are the same kids. If they drove you crazy while they were in school, they still will . . . only all day long!

We all know that we need to change. We know that we should be more patient and understanding, more firm and consistent. We know that we need to be more organized and more in control of what goes on in our homes. As Christians, we know we are supposed to be growing more like Christ as we grow in the Lord.

Do you want to change? Are you willing to do things differently? Then home schooling may be just what you want! If you really want to grow, teaching your kids at home will add plenty of extra pressure to your weak points. You will either become a better woman or a worse one. You will learn more than your kids will. You don't have to be perfect to home school . . . you just must be willing to improve. Your kids will learn more from your example than from your chosen curriculum. You have the opportunity to teach them that one should never stop growing and learning!

This book is to help everyday people like us do a good job home schooling our children. I hope you find it very practical.

Yes, real people do this!

2

What Will the Neighbors (and My Mother-in-Law) Think?

"It's kind of like building an ark in your backyard and hoping your neighbors won't notice!"
— Rae Holtzendorff, home schooling mom

Y ou will encounter many different responses to your decision to home school. Some will laud you as a brave, angelic supermom and others will think you are nuts. I have found that the general public, with the exception of an occasional schoolteacher, are very positive toward the idea. A few think it's a good thing, but worry that the children will grow up to be odd.

It seems the ones who most often have a negative reaction to home teaching are those who feel some responsibility for the kids, such as grandparents, neighbors, and the people at church. These people know you well enough to remember some of the dumb things you've done in the past. They may have reason to worry . . . Therefore listen and prayerfully consider whatever they may have to say.

On the other hand, it is common for people to feel threatened by anyone who is doing something different. Some friends and associates may assume that you think they are less spiritual or less caring parents if they do not choose to home teach. Your own parents may see your decision to keep your kids at home as a reflection of your inner feelings about the choices they made as you were growing up. When people feel threatened by your "radical plans," they may need to come up with reasons why what you are doing is a bad idea, so they will feel justified in not doing it themselves. Give them the freedom to hold and express their opinions. Try not to make it an issue. You are the parents and in the end it is your decision, but it *is* important to be kind and to respect the ideas of others. People are especially offended by statements like those in the following section. Even if it *is* how you really feel, refrain from saying so and avoid the strife and misunderstanding which would follow . . .

Rash Statements to Avoid

❑ "As a Christian, I could never send my children to public school!"

❑ "God has only given parents the job of teaching their children."

❑ "I plan to home school clear through high school."

❑ "I don't want my children with all those other kids."

❑ (To your parents) "I don't want my kids to go through what I went through."

❑ "College isn't important. I want her to be a good wife and mother."

Family

Another thing to remember is that at times our parents and in-laws have their own problems with peer pressure. They have to consider what they will tell their friends when asked where their grandchildren go to school. If everyone thinks you are crazy, it is a reflection on them. Many have a genuine concern for the education of their grandchildren. This is one reason it is helpful to join an established home school "school." Then your parents can tell their friends that the kids go to "Such and Such Christian School," thus avoiding any potentially embarrassing questions. They will also feel better if they know that someone "who knows something about education" is supervising your home school.

They probably want your children to go on to college and be "successful' in life. These things are important to them because they care. If they sent you to college, they will be sensitive to how much you value your own education. You should respect their feelings even if you don't see everything the same way. Allow them to see that your goals for the kids are pretty much the same . . . you really care about their future success too. Most grandparents will give you at least one school year to prove yourself. Here are some guidelines:

- ❏ Don't commit yourself for more than a year at a time . . . Figure that you can't do too much damage in a year. It is wise to plan ahead, but foolish to announce what you will do in the future (James 4:13,14).

- ❏ Don't make rash statements. (See preceding section!)

- ❏ Describe your plans in a way that is socially acceptable to your parents. Consider becoming part of an established home school program so that there will be some accountability.

❏ Don't try to talk anyone into home schooling.

❏ Be open . . . Don't act guilty or sneaky . . . You're not selling drugs . . .

❏ Don't talk too much about it. Give short answers to questions . . . They were probably just being polite.

❏ Thank people for advice, comments and observations. Thank God for those who offer it!

❏ Be interested in and enthusiastic about what other people are doing with their kids . . . home schooling or not.

❏ Remember, God not only created us to be unique individuals, He also sometimes deals with us in unique ways. Give others the freedom to follow God in what may seem to us a different direction.

Neighbors

Some of the same advice applies to your neighbors, but here are a few more tips. Remember to be a good neighbor! Your overall testimony in your neighborhood will go a long way toward determining what the response will be when they suspect your kids aren't in school. Here is a quiz:

❏ Do you know your neighbors?

❏ Do you keep your yard neat?

❏ Do you keep your pets from annoying your neighbors?

❏ Do your children respect other people and their property?

❏ Do your neighbors perceive you as friendly and open?

❏ Have you refrained from taking sides in neighborhood disputes?

❏ Are you a peacemaker?

If the answer to any of these questions is "No," then you are more likely to get a hostile response.

One of the ladies in our home school group has a sister who lives in the same neighborhood with another home schooling family. She hoped that they weren't part of our group. "Those kids are in the street all day," she said "They ride down the middle of the street and obstruct traffic. They make a lot of noise and I can't figure out when they *ever* do any schoolwork!" The neighbor was probably justified in her concern, and the home school mom should have had more control over her kids and their schedule.

In this situation, it was what the neighbors *observed* that made them critical of the home schooling family. Perhaps the criticism is valid, perhaps not; but if they don't know you, don't feel free to talk to you, and are concerned about what they see, they may just call the authorities . . .

Such calls are not always provoked, however. We have one neighbor whose hobby appears to be reporting the rest of the neighborhood for any possible infraction of a city ordinance. One day after lunch, a little oriental lady drove up and parked in front of my house. As she approached my door with a briefcase and a handful of papers, I went to meet her, my children spilling out the door behind me. "Hi! May I help you?" "Yes, I'm Mrs. Chou from Child Welfare Services," she said," and I am here to investigate a report that you are doing unlicensed child care in your home." I invited her in and explained that I cared for my own children in my home. Was there a problem with that? "No, not at all," she replied, "but what about the other children? You see, it is really a very simple procedure to obtain a license." I explained again that these were *my* children, but she didn't get it . . . She probably thought only 2.5 of the kids were mine. Finally I said, "There are seven children here. I personally have given birth to each of them, and they all have the same father, who is my husband. They live here all the time and I take care of them. Sometimes a friend will leave her kids with me while she goes to the store, but other than that, it's only my own children, many though they are. Do I need a license for that?" She laughed and said no, I didn't need a license for my own kids. She thanked me for being kind and patient and said that many people became so angry! I said that I guessed I had no reason to be angry, since I was not doing anything wrong. She was a sweet lady . . . We had a nice visit and she never even asked why all those kids weren't at school at 1:30 in the afternoon.

Hiding the kids in the house from 8:00 to 3:00 isn't the whole answer, but it would be wise to keep regular hours. It is a good idea to know when the other kids on your block come home from school. Some days when I simply *must* get some errands run, we have "rolling schoolhouse" in the van. If we are out in the early afternoon and someone asks about it, the kids and I say, "We have half-day." The fact that we have half-day everyday doesn't make it any less true.

Let's face it . . . we *do* judge a book by its cover, more often than not, and so will your neighbors. If they see you as a caring parent, good neighbor and a responsible citizen, they will feel that you not only know what you are doing, but that you are doing your children a favor. In fact, they may even ask you to teach their children! This has happened to a number of moms in our group.

To sum it up, if *we* behave in a Christ-like manner, few people will question our decision to teach our children (to be Christ-like) at home, right? Christ instructed us to love our neighbor as ourselves. Who is our neighbor? It is our parents, our friends, the people in our neighborhoods. It is our brothers and sisters and uncles and cousins. It is really anyone with whom we have contact . . . even the truant officer and school officials.

We find out how this love is supposed to behave as we read 1 Corinthians 13.

Love is patient, love is kind and is not jealous; love does not brag and is not arrogant, does not act unbecomingly; it does not seek its own, is not provoked, does not take into account a wrong suffered, does not rejoice in unrighteousness, but rejoices with the truth; bears all things, hopes all things, endures all things.

In Galatians 5 we are given another description of a Christian.

But the fruit of the Spirit is love, joy, peace, patience, kindness, goodness, faithfulness, gentleness and self-control; against such things there is no law.

In other words, no one can legitimately get upset with that kind of behavior!

We are usually not persecuted for our faith so much as for the failure to live out our faith. Let your decision to home teach motivate you to become more like the Lord Jesus. Are there attitudes and habits that others see, or even that they don't see, which are inconsistent with the character of Christ? Be willing to confess these as sin and ask the Lord to help you as you purpose to change.

The Law

If the legal status of home schooling in your state is still up in the air, we urge you to obtain legal insurance from the Home School Legal Defense Association. The fee is reasonable, and if you are contacted by the authorities, it will be the best money you ever spent.

Even if you never are contacted, it is a good investment in the freedom of home schoolers all over the country. Whenever a home schooling case goes to court, it affects everyone within jurisdiction of the court. If a case ever goes to the Supreme Court, it will affect all of us. Under this insurance, we can all have excellent, likeminded constitutional lawyers available to defend us. It is important to remember that together we are only as strong as the weakest link in the home school chain. Send for information and application forms to:

Home School Legal Defense Association
P.O. Box 2091
Washington, D.C. 20013

For current information on the legal status of home schooling in your state, write to the above address, or call (202) 546-2335. These attorneys and their staff love the Lord. They believe in and practice home schooling themselves. They are there to help us avoid and, when necessary, win any legal battles that come our way.

What will the neighbors think? It's mainly up to us. Of course, it *does* help if we know what we are doing! With this in mind, let's take a look at the nitty-gritty (and seldom revealed) realities of home schooling.

3

What About Time for Me?

"He is no fool who gives up what he cannot keep, to keep that which he cannot lose."
— Jim Elliot, Christian missionary and martyr

"You only go around once in life, so grab for all the gusto you can get!"
— Beer commercial

T-I-M-E. What is it? We say that time is money because it has real value, but we don't say that money is time, because you can't horde it or save it for a rainy day. The rich and the poor have equal amounts in each day, and we all choose how it will be used.

We spend time the way we want to. We appreciate it when someone spends time with us. We spend a lot of time worrying, or in front of the mirror or in front of the television. We spend time in prayer or with our friends or with our family. We are hurt when someone special doesn't have time for us. We pay doctors to give us time in their day. We are very irritated when we have to waste our time in a waiting room or in a nonproductive meeting.

Why is time so precious? Because time is what our lives are made of. When we die, our time here is up. While we live, it is how we spend our time that will govern who we really are and what impact we will have had on the world when we are gone. Whether we owned or rented our houses, lived in the good or bad section of town, wore nice clothes or not, were pretty or plain, will not matter at all after we are gone. How we chose to spend our time will matter long after we are gone. If we wasted most of it, it will matter in what was not accomplished. If we spent time with eternity in mind, it will matter for eternity.

This does not mean that we must spend our lives in frenzied activity. We just need to think through what our options are and spend the bulk of our time and energy on what matters most in the long run. This means taking the time to read God's Word and find out what is important in His economy. How often we spend fifteen minutes ranting and raving about spilled milk which won't matter at all day after tomorrow, and then we ignore the kids when they are outright disobedient because we are busy spending time on "something important." We need to be judicious in our use of time.

In choosing to teach your own kids full-time, you are making a choice *not* to do certain other things that you may enjoy doing. Most women's Bible study programs do not provide child care for school-age children. You can't go to the gym and work out unless you go very early or have teenagers. If you want to go out of town for a week, who will teach the kids? It is harder to get your other jobs, like laundry and housework, done. I usually end up doing my shopping at night after dinner. I am not trying to talk you out of it, I am just being realistic.

On the other hand, no one is forcing me to do this. This is the choice I have made. I have considered all the options for the use of my time and I have decided to use it to home school my children. It is still my time. No one has stolen it. I control the use of it.

We live in a society in which we are taught that pleasure and "fun" are the chief end of man. We are encouraged to be selfish and narcissistic, to "look out for number one." People who live a life of giving, like Mother Theresa, are considered very special by the world, but "only a saint could live like that."

Women's magazines are full of articles about women who found themselves 'losing their identity' in the daily humdrum of wiping little noses, fixing meals and doing laundry. The only solution for such a woman, of course, is to break the bonds, brave the reproach of her husband and bewilderment of the kids, go to college and find out Who She Really Is. Then she can get a job that not only earns money, but gives her the satisfaction of knowing that she is Really Helping People. The article goes on to say that her kids are probably better off now and her husband is proud of her . . . or her husband left, but he was just too insecure and the marriage couldn't have lasted anyway. We are being told that we are not really who we are unless we see ourselves in a context other than that of a wife and mother.

There *are* a lot of things I want to do in my lifetime. I couldn't spend my whole life home schooling my kids even if I wanted to. Since my youngest is four and I have already been doing this for five years, I may do it longer than most, but I have a list of things I would like to pursue when I am finished home teaching. As I look at my life, I see that there are some things that can *only* be done now, if they are to be done at all, and that there are other things that can wait until later.

I found out that when my kids turned five and went to school, they disappeared! I didn't have much time with them anymore and what time I had, I could not call "quality" time. I don't know about you, but mornings before the kids left for school were usually not pleasant. There are lunches to make, breakfast to oversee, we are probably out of milk, there are lost shoes, mismatched socks, unbrushed teeth, homework lost or neglected, and the parting shot is usually, "You're going to be late!"

When they get home it is not a whole lot better. They bring in with them all kinds of emotional baggage that I have no idea what to do with or where it came from. One child has had a spat with a best friend, another thinks he was treated unfairly by his teacher, one is higher than a kite from eating someone's Twinkies at lunch, and another flunked a spelling test. Then they take out all their aggressions on each other, the mother and the dog.

They also have homework. Ugh! After six hours at school, there is more work to do. The kids are tired and Mom is tired. Helping with homework is rarely quality time. Usually I haven't the foggiest notion why this work was assigned. Is this extra work? Is it work that should have been done in class? Why does my child not understand this!? What does the teacher want? How has this been taught? When I try to explain it, all I get is, "That's not the way my teacher said to do it!" (It is easier to home school than to help with homework.)

When that ordeal is over, they want to *play!* So out the door they go to spend time with their friends from school or in the neighborhood. They return for dinner, chores and possibly more homework, then leave for church meetings, Boy Scouts, soccer practice, ad infinitum. If there is a TV involved, it also gets a share, and then to bed.

When do *I* get time with them? I could make them stay home on Saturdays: "No, you may not go to that birthday party. You have to stay home so I can influence you." That would go over like a lead balloon.

Now that I am home teaching my kids, I get them during prime time. I get them first. After spending the better part of the day with them, I don't mind if they want to go play with their friends in the neighborhood. In fact, I'm ready! I know what they did all day, I had a big part in making it happen. I *know* my kids. We have lived and worked together . . . I have taught them and shared my life with them . . . I like them. They are people that, for the most part, I really enjoy spending time with.

My oldest is sixteen. The time I have had with him I will never have again in the same way. Time goes by very rapidly. In ten more years, if the Lord tarries, I will be only forty-six and my youngest almost fifteen. I will have plenty of time to do other things if the Lord gives me the time, and if He doesn't, I didn't need it anyway!. My time is something I can give my children now in a way that I won't be able to give them later. It is time that I can be with them and teach them godly values. I can use situations in our every-day life to illustrate Biblical truth. I will never have this time again. Many things can wait, but kids grow up.

What are the dividends of teaching your kids at home? First of all, I receive a lot of personal fulfill-ment. I think I have what so many women are looking for in jobs outside the home and are not finding. I am challenged every day to use wisdom and reasoning powers. I use my mind all the time and I am learning new things every day. Not only are my math skills in better working order than they have ever been, but I am learning about things in American history I'd never heard before. Now that I am an adult, none of it is bor-ing. I am learning teaching skills that will be useful all my life, and I have the joy of seeing measurable per-sonal growth both mentally and spiritually. I see the Lord working on my weak spots everyday, making me more conformed to the image of Christ.

Secondly, I am able to share special times with my kids that would be impossible if they were not at home with me or I at home with them. The older ones and I share knowing looks and laughter at the funny things the little ones do and say. We have time to have long talks about serious subjects when the time is just right. I give them tips on parenting and driving and choosing a mate as we go about our normal routine. I am on-the-spot to teach the children how to get along with each other, and to explain to them how these skills will help them as adults.

We can talk about what the Lord is doing in our family. We make up family jokes, we tickle each other and laugh together. We read Bible stories, ask questions of each other and pray together. These are things that non-home schoolers also enjoy, but perhaps not as often.

All these things happen, but not every day. For this reason you need to see your commitment in terms of at least a year at a time. Gold seekers squatted on creek banks for months, sifting through tons of mud and sand in order to find one nugget. I challenge you to "go for the gold"!

Now, let's get down to brass tacks. Have you really given thought to how you spend your time? Home schooling involves giving up certain things and rearranging your schedule and priorities, just as any job does.

I talked to a lady recently whose husband was very excited about home schooling. He was also very supportive and helpful—so long as she did a wonderful job of home teaching. She is an immaculate housekeeper and loves to iron. Her kids play baseball and soccer and take ballet and music lessons. They make a big fuss and make her feel guilty if she goes anywhere without them, even to the grocery store, so, even though she has a teenage daughter, they all go everywhere with her. She and her husband rarely go out alone, but she does go one day a week to a women's Bible study. It is this study that is holding her together. She has gotten to the point where she hates home teaching and can hardly stand the sight of her kids. This makes her feel like a failure as a mother, so she is even less able to say "No" to them. It is a vicious cycle. At some point she needs to decide *where* she wants to spend her time, then eliminate what doesn't fit. Something has got to give—either some of the children's demands and activities, or the home teaching.

On the other hand, I know another lady with a different problem. She has many friends and spends a lot of time on the phone. She loves to do crafts and is very good at it. She has been involved in a craft boutique every year at Christmastime, and must spend a great deal of time preparing for it in the fall. She struggles with her laundry and housework and is never caught up. They all like to sleep in. If she can't get away from the house and the kids one morning a week, she feels like she will go crazy. Many days home schooling just doesn't happen. Her kids are rapidly falling behind academically. Several things have got to change if home schooling is going to work in this family. Consideration needs to be given as to what *is* being taught in this home. This is a situation where the kids might be better off in school if the mom can't change.

In order to lead a productive life we must learn to do our work before we play. How can we tell our kids that they must get their schoolwork done before they can play if we sit in a messy house so intent on our hobbies that we forget to fix dinner?

When I looked at the demands on my time, I decided to eliminate sports and lessons and women's daytime Bible studies from my schedule. My kids aren't really into sports, and I console myself with the fact that the pioneers did OK without ballet and music lessons.

As for my own personal recreation time, my husband and I have a standing date every Friday night. This is very important to us. I also often take a friend grocery shopping with me when I go at night. This turns a chore into a ladies' night out. From time to time I read a good book. I love to read, but have trouble getting anything else done until I finish the book, so I hold off as long as I can, and then read late at night. This makes me rather grumpy and groggy the next day, but to me it's worth it!

Here are some ideas that may help you:

❑ Realize that home teaching is a job. You are now employed at least part-time away from your usual household duties. It *will* be harder to get the other stuff done. If you think of what your life would be like if you worked outside your home four hours a day, you will have a better picture of what to expect. There is one difference, however: when you are at work and the kids are at school or a sitter's, no one is at home messing everything up!

As in any other job, you will have a few wonderful days when you feel like you are a real success, some when you feel like a total failure and wonder whatever possessed you to do this, and the rest will be rather humdrum and routine, once you get the hang of it.

❑ Avoid reading women's magazines and articles that create discontent. Just as we believe that our children's input should be monitored, we should be careful about what we expose ourselves to also. Read books and articles that support the family and draw you closer to the Lord and His goals for our lives.

❑ Teach your children to respect your privacy and time alone. This is especially true if you are more of an introvert. Introverts refuel their emotional tanks by being alone, whereas extroverts refuel by being with people. Keep this in mind as you figure out what to do for relaxation. For many people, just being with other human beings all the time with no break is exhausting, and children are especially demanding human beings. Make the kids understand that when your bedroom door is closed, they *may not* come in or disturb you unless there is a real emergency. I tell my children, do not disturb me unless some one is bleeding . . . badly! If you have little ones, I recommend daily rest times. Putting the little ones down for a nap and having the older ones on their beds for an hour of looking at books or quiet play, has worked well for me.

Take time to be alone to think, read and spend time in the Word and in prayer. Take time to collect your thoughts, write a letter or take a nap. Once they learn to respect this time, you will find it easier to give your kids the rest of the time.

❏ Teach them to respect your time away from them. As home schooling moms, we are not the ones who leave our kids in day care all the time while we go gadding about. No— in fact, the kids seem omnipresent! For this reason it is a good idea for you to leave them with Grandma or a sitter, and spend some time with some adults from time to time.

Our children need to understand that as adults, we have lives of our own, and that we do not exist merely as their caretakers. Our husbands need some individual attention too, and we need it from them. I want my children to see how important Ed and I are to each other. If they see my husband taking me on dates, my sons will learn that that is what husbands are supposed to do! Their wives will thank us! I want my daughters to learn bal ance from me so that mothering will be easier for them.

The other reason I leave my kids in the care of others from time to time is that I want them to know that they can do all right without me. I have a friend who had two boys whom she never left. They went with her everywhere, and had never even spent the night at Grandma's. She was diagnosed as having cancer and had to spend six weeks in the hospital. It was terrible for her children. They did not know that someone else could take care of them. It was more traumatic for them than it would have been if they had been used to having others care for them. My friend lived and had another baby boy. He along with his brothers were left with a sitter or Grandma on occasion, and they are all well-adjusted and in college now. (Just thought you'd want to know.)

❏ Decide what has to be eliminated from your life in order to bring in home schooling. I'm not sure what it is like in other parts of the country, but I hear' that we who live in Southern California are even more frenzied in our activities than in other places. Here is a list of the various things that some ladies have laid aside for the time being.

> Evening adult education classes
> Church choir
> Window shopping
> Doll making
> Sunday school teaching
> Ironing
> Gourmet cooking
> Tole painting
> Women's Bible study
> Hang gliding
> Selling Avon
> Coffee klatches
> Lunch with the girls

❏ Decide what you *really* want to do for your growth and enjoyment. Figure out where it is in your priorities, then *make time* for it in your life. See above list for some possibilities.

All this to say that you *are* in charge of your time, whether you take charge of it or not. The Lord has given us our lives to spend with our free will. He spent His life in service and sacrifice on our behalf. He said, *"He who saves his life shall lose it, and he who loses his life for my sake, he it is who finds it."* He also set an example for us when He went away by Himself from time to time to be alone with God.

As mothers, let's go to Jesus and seek His priorities. He will help us find balance in our lives.

4

What Do the Daddies Do?

*"Sure, Honey, if that's
what you want to do,
it's okay with me."*
— Husband of home schooling mom

First of all I think it is important to point out that God has given our children two parents for a reason. God has also clearly stated in His Word that the husband is the head of the house and in the position to direct what goes on there. This applies whether your husband is a fervent believer, a tepid hearer-but-not-doer, or an outright unbeliever. There is no indication in the Bible that the father's spiritual status, or lack of it, makes any difference in his position in the home. If your husband is dead set against home teaching his children, it is safe to assume God doesn't think you ought to do it either. Ladies, if you want the blessing of the Lord on this endeavor, don't go over your husband's head!

Some fathers are unsure about the idea and have a hard time figuring out what they will tell their friends at work, but often they will give their wives a year to try it out. Often these men become the most ardent supporters of home schooling and are very proud of their wives as time goes on. Others concede that it works and give permission for one more year.

Much has been said about the husband's role in home schooling. I feel that much of what has been said is not very realistic. Often the men who write these articles are employed at home, have jobs with flexible hours or aren't even married. These articles can make a husband feel inadequate and his wife feel discontented since her husband doesn't "measure up." After all, he doesn't take his kids to work three days a week or teach them astronomy. He doesn't stick around in the morning to read the Bible or conduct devotions every night. He is not all that interested in the kids' schoolwork, or in teaching them to rebuild an engine, and would rather mow the lawn than do flash cards.

Although some men are very uninvolved with their children in general, and home schooling hasn't changed that, I would say that the majority of home schooling fathers are above average in their fathering skills.

My husband is a godly man and he is very supportive of home schooling. He takes his God given responsibilities to his family seriously. He is not, however, "involved in home schooling" the way some say he ought to be.

First of all, he is at work nine hours a day earning enough money so that I can stay at home and teach our kids. I think this is a very important part of the overall home schooling picture! In doing so he is setting a good example of faithfulness and responsibility to our kids as he goes to work every day, even when he would rather stay at home with us. He is the one who enables me to fulfill the role of the traditional stay-at-home wife and mother. There are many women who have to go to work every day just to support their husband's hobbies. I am blessed to have a man who has different priorities for my time.

Secondly, he takes good care of me! He tells me I am wonderful, and that I am doing a good job. He doesn't question my abilities, but rather encourages me in what I am trying to do. He listens to me when I have had a bad day or a bad week, and is sympathetic rather than critical. He takes me out on a date almost every Friday night, and doesn't fuss about watching the kids so I can go out with a friend from time to time.

Lastly, he plays with the kids when he is home. They wrestle all over the living room floor, and the kids stick to him like barnacles. He is gentle and never makes them cry by teasing them or playing too rough. At least once a week he reads aloud to the middle kids, usually for longer than an hour. He often reads to the little boys and prays with them and puts them to bed. He enjoys singing to the girls and praying with them before bed. He helps the older boys fix their bikes and likes to play strategy games with them from time to time.

Every dad is different, just as every mom is different. Each family is different just as every child is different. We all are called to be obedient to the Lord and to become conformed to the image of Christ. Christ is our standard, not a man-made list of "ought to's." The Bible doesn't say that fathers must be involved in teaching academic subjects, or even in teaching their children their trade.

What the Bible *does* say is:

> *Love the Lord your God with all your heart and with all your soul and with all your strength. These commandments that I give you today are to be upon your hearts. Impress them on your children. Talk about them when you sit at home and when you walk along the road, when you lie down and when you get up."*

This standard is harder to keep. It involves living it rather than completing a set of prescribed activities. A man may read the Bible at breakfast and do family devotions and yet not love the Lord his God with all his heart, soul and strength. A man who loves the Lord with all his heart, soul and strength may not do those things, but may have a far greater impact in the lives of his family than one who does. It is a man's heart for God that impresses the commandments on the hearts of his children. If a man has a heart for God, he will naturally talk about it at home and as he walks (or drives) along the road and when he lies down and rises up.

Children grow up to be well-rounded Christians when they see their parents really living the Christian life. Parents who don't practice what they preach have children who question the validity of Christianity no matter where the kids go to school or how many times the Bible is read in the home. My grandfather read the Bible to the family every morning at breakfast until the day he died. We are not sure whether he was a believer or not, and my dad did not trust Christ until he was an adult.

My parents trusted Christ as their Savior when I was four years old. At some point during the next year, I too asked the Lord to forgive my sins and make me a child of God. As my parents grew in the Lord, our home life became an extension of their Christianity. We did not have regular Bible reading or "family devotions" as such. My dad read aloud to us often. He read *Grimm's Fairy Tales*, *Robinson Crusoe*, missionary stories, and Bible stories. One of my parents prayed with each of us before we went to sleep at night.

I grew up having never heard my mother or father say a mean, hurtful or sarcastic word to each other. They still stand in the kitchen and smooch like they did while I was growing up. When Daddy came home from work, he acted as though his real day had just begun. He wasn't too grumpy or tired to kiss Mom, play with us, or read stories.

We never got any lectures on "what Christians must or must not do." They just lived it. My parents became sponsors of the college group at our church when I was about eight years old. We had Bible studies and parties at our house all the time. It seemed that every Sunday there were a few college boys who were tired of dorm food and who came home with us to eat. Although we didn't have much money, we could always divide the potatoes and cut the pot roast a little thinner.

We got to know these college kids. My folks discussed what was going on in their lives as we sat at the dinner table. "Patty is dating a non-Christian and won't listen to reason. She is losing her zeal for the Lord." "Tom is interested in going to the mission field and doesn't know whether to try to find a wife first." "Fred is out of school and without a job. He is spending his days in prayer, while living at home, wondering what God's will is for his life." And so on. We watched them all come and go, succeed and fail, grow in the Lord or fall into sin or some strange doctrine. We *saw* what was right and wrong. We also saw how God's Word speaks to life's everyday problems.

When I was about eight or nine my dad started going down to Los Angeles on Friday and Saturday nights to do street preaching with Open Air Campaigners. I went with him a number of times and was able to share Christ with people down there. He often brought very strange people home to sleep on our living room floor, so that they could attend church with us the next day. There were Marines, actors, members of the Mafia, stuntmen, people from other countries and some real wackos. My sisters and I have some very unique memories of these people! But it was all very interesting and exciting to us and seemed normal, although I think we did suspect that we had more fun than most kids.

My dad was an oil salesman and drove a pick-up truck all over the L.A. basin from one gas station to another. It was wonderful to hear at the dinner table each night about Daddy's adventures. He had many opportunities to share the Lord with people as he went, and we loved to hear his stories. We still have our favorites . . . We get him to tell them again from time to time.

The three of us girls went to public school until I was in the fourth grade. I led several of my playmates to the Lord, my mom had a Good News Club in our living room once a week, my middle sister led our youngest sister to Christ. She in turn led two or three kids to the Lord on the bus going to kindergarten. One of these still keeps in touch with my youngest sister as her "spiritual mother." We each had our turn sharing at the dinner table about these things, as well as the normal events of the day.

In short, we were raised by example to believe that there is no more interesting or exciting place to be than where God is at work in people's lives. None of us rebelled and all of us find our greatest joy in serving the Lord in various ways.

How should fathers be involved in home schooling? Not by following some man-made standard, but by being obedient to the Word of God. Make Christ your standard in the way you conduct yourself in your relationships with your kids, your wife, your neighbors and the people at work. Ask these questions: "How would the Lord respond to this?" "What would He say?" "How would He say it?" You're not sure? Go to the Word and find out. Let the Holy Spirit speak to you about how you spend your time and money. Let God change you. Tell your children what God is doing in your life. Work through your decisions out loud so they can see how a man of God makes decisions, and responds to problems. Admit your faults. Tell how the sermon on Sunday applies to *your* life. In other words, live your relationship with God before your family. Show them what Jesus is like.

When my kids wonder about their Heavenly Father, they should rest in the knowledge that He is like their Daddy. When they think of Heaven, it should comfort them to know that it is just like home, only better.

Climbing Mount Never-Rest

*"There was an old woman
who lived in a shoe,
She had so many helpers,
She didn't know what to do!"*
— Mother Goose, paraphrased

"She rises also . . .and gives prescribed tasks to her maidens."
— Proverbs 31

P robably the biggest problem for the home schooling mom is how to get all the other stuff done now that she is spending hours each day teaching her kids. Not only are we faced with the same situation as mothers who work outside the home with respect to limited time, but we also have little mess-makers chasing us around all day, undoing our work! In this chapter I will address some housework bugaboos, one at a time.

I want you to know right at the beginning that in this area I am *extra* normal. I have read all those "get your act together" books with little effect. I have a friend who wrote one of those books. She wanted to try out her theories on me while she was writing it, figuring I was the acid test. The book almost didn't get written.

I tend to be, well, rather unstructured in my approach. I just about went under during the first three years, trying to keep up with home schooling five kids, chasing two toddlers, running our home school group and doing the housework. I am not a slob, and my house is not filthy. I just drown in paper piles and can't keep current on all the various facets of housework at once. It is hard for me to choose to wash a floor (which will be dirty again ten minutes from now) over people who need my help.

But the Lord is so good. He knows what He is doing. He gave me a wonderful husband who can't feel relaxed or have fun unless the house is tidy. This has made me much more aware of the condition of things than I normally would be, and I have definitely improved over the years. My job descriptions, however, have been multiplying whereas my managerial skills have been increasing by simple addition.

All this is to say that I don't speak from authority, but rather from experience. I am not a victor, but a survivor. I have tried many approaches to the various aspects of housework with varying results. From me, you will get more sympathy than help. Since there is no *real* help, and we get so little sympathy, you should find this chapter very refreshing.

Laundry

The problem with laundry is that people keep changing clothes! You know, in the olden days people wore the same clothes all week (and longer in the winter) and the women just changed aprons. That's why they were able to get along without washing machines. Of course they didn't have phones, cars, piano lessons and doctor's appointments to keep them hopping either!. Can you imagine my laundry for nine people? I have also had three bed-wetters to keep up with. This is what my husband calls "Mount Never-rest." Often I would get several loads of laundry clean and sometimes even folded, but not quite put away. When someone would *need* something . . . yes, you guessed it . . . what they wanted was not on the top. In no time it would all be knocked onto the floor! Of course the floor is where I had all the dirty laundry waiting, right? Back to square one . . .

Have you ever put all the clothes that needed folding on your bed, saying to yourself, "There! Now it will have to be done before I go to bed tonight!" Of course, the reason we *have* bedspreads is so that we can gather up the laundry in them and dump it all on the floor when bedtime comes! Yes, the Scriptures are true when they say, *"The heart of man is deceitful above all things . . .".*

I have tried many different methods for getting the laundry done. Some of these may work better for you than they have for me if you have fewer kids or a more organized life, or both. I will list various ideas; I recommend that you try them and see which ones work best for you.

❏ Each child has his own color of laundry basket in his room. Into this basket he places his laundry and takes it to the laundry area when you tell him to. When the clothes are clean, you put them in his basket, either folded, or ready for him to fold, and he puts them away.

❏ Each child has his own laundry day. On this day he brings his clothes and takes care of all the washing, drying and folding of his own clothes. This is after you have instructed him how to use the machinery involved, of course. The disadvantage of this system is that the kids forget that they have something in the washer or dryer, and when it's your turn, the machines are still occupied. A timer is helpful to remind them when it is time for a change.

❑ You have certain times each day when you get in the habit of processing the laundry. For example, before breakfast, during lunch, and while dinner is cooking. This can work well with idea #1.

❑ Make it one child's chore to sort and fold socks, another's to fold towels and help do the sheets. Older kids can put the younger kids clothes away, as well as their own.

❑ Here is a great one: Mark your kids' clothes with dots. One dot for the oldest boy and or oldest girl, two dots for the second, etc.. This way when they are outgrown and handed down to the next child, all you have to do is add a dot. This way someone besides you can properly sort your clothes.

❑ Call the local laundry service to get a price for your kind of volume so that you know how much your time is worth. Don't tell the kids; they might get ideas about a home business.

❑ On the other hand, if you have an older child who would like to be gainfully employed, with a little proper training, you may have a wonderful solution to the laundry blues.

Cleaning the Kitchen Floor

One of the problems I have had with keeping the kitchen floor clean is that the only time there is no one on it is while we are all upstairs having school. I know that some of you do your regular mopping when the kids are in bed, and for some this works well, especially if the kids are down by 8:00 P.M. I have several reasons why this is not a good idea for me; my kids stay up too late, the lighting in the kitchen is poor, and I am too tired by that time and I want to visit with my husband.

I have found that my kids may do well with cleaning bathrooms, emptying trash, feeding animals, and dusting around things, but it is not worth it to have them mop! There are too many variables. It seems that there is always either too much soap, too much water, or not enough sweeping ahead of time or rinsing afterward. I have five boys, and I think that there is something having to do with male genes that makes them *unable* to see dirt on floors. I can *always* sweep after they do and come up with a pile.

What works best is to just do it at regular intervals and know in your heart of hearts that it is cleaner, even if they march across it ten minutes later and it looks the same as it did before. After all, they didn't stick to it as they went through!

Kids' Chores (Inside Help)

Most home school books present child labor as a meaningful part of home education as well as the solution to the problems that arise when the mother takes on another full-time in-home job. It is true that learning the value of work is part of growing up to be a responsible adult and that industry and resourcefulness should be encouraged. But, *"All that glistens is not gold,"* quoth the Bard.

We are sinners and our children are sinners and I think it really shows up in the area of chores. I have found that *no* system ever works for more than a month or so. We must keep coming up with new plans, whips, and carrots to keep the little donkeys moving. The other problem is that it takes more effort to keep them doing the work than it would to do the job myself. I tend to taper off until the whole new plan slides into oblivion because I lack the discipline to do *my* job (making them do their job) whenever it needs doing.

It is not so much that children are disobedient about doing their chores. It is usually that they are childish and are much better at only remembering what they want to remember than we are. They can be told, "Every morning before breakfast you must feed the rabbit," but if we don't remind them, it doesn't happen. Since we would feel bad if the rabbit died, we keep it alive by reminding the kid. I suppose that a natural consequence would be to leave the animal to the mercy of the child after a good lecture on the subject.

Another problem is that children don't have a complete picture of what needs to be accomplished in a given job. For example, they will scrub the sink and make it very "clean," but leave it full of cleanser, with a rag on the back of the toilet and a puddle on the floor. This problem can be solved with proper training, but it needs to be *"line upon line, precept upon precept . . ."* again and again and again. Even after all this careful and *patient* training, quality control is constantly needed for satisfactory results.

The other great agony of chores is that even when kids are being obedient and careful, they are so distractible that you can never count on the job being done in any reasonable amount of time. The problem is intensified when company is coming, or when school starts after the work is done. There have been times when I thought that my kids would only be well prepared for life as domiciliary help, since they spent so much time on it, and comparatively little on "school."

I have yet to find a mother who is really happy with her system. A lot of fathers are also frustrated with their wives' seeming inability to manage the children. These men have some very interesting theories as to how it ought to be done. Let's face it, mothers are mothers and fathers are fathers and they each have different ways of relating to and dealing with the children. I firmly believe that God is the one who made it this way. Most kids would be a mess if they were raised full-time by their fathers, and it is questionable if the fathers would even survive at all! On the other hand, we mothers are relieved and amazed to see our little rascals "hop to" when Daddy says the word. It gives us hope for the children, and it makes us respect our men for their ability to take charge.

Now for some good ideas and assorted plans of attack. None of them will work forever, but variety is the spice of life. Changing the game plan keeps everyone on their toes and teaches flexibility.

❑ "Chore of the day" plan. Each child is required to do his regular personal care-taking (brush hair, make bed, brush teeth, get dressed, etc.) as appropriate to his age. In addition to that, he is assigned one household chore, keyed to their abilities and my schedule. For example, if I am going to have time to supervise, and if we will be home all day, maybe my eight-year-old would wash, dry, fold and put away a load of towels. (We don't often have those kind of days.) On a normal day (i.e., moderately hectic) she might be required to sweep the front porch. On a very busy day, we would forget about children's chores altogether.

❑ The "Work with Mom" plan. Each child spends a period of time (15-30 minutes) working with Mom on whatever chores she needs to do. This plan has the advantage of time spent together, and opportunities for thorough training. The main drawback is fitting it into my schedule! Too many days I am in a hurry and I need to do it myself if it is going to get done in time. On days when we are on the go, it is nearly impossible to make this plan work.

❑ The rotating chore plan. This is good for a large family. There is a list of chores that need to be done. For example:

Job A: Clear table after each meal and load dishwasher and run as needed, scour kitchen sink Monday Wednesday and Friday.

Job B: Put chairs on table and sweep after dinner, vacuum living room on Monday and Friday.

Job C: Feed and water animals every day and carry out all the trash daily.

Job D: Clean bathrooms on Monday and Friday, water lawns Tuesday and Saturday.

Each child has a different job each week on a rotating schedule. The beauty of this program is that no one has the job he hates for more than a week at a time, and no one can say, "You give him all the easy jobs!" If you will look again, you will notice that the kids are working in different parts of the house, so they are less likely to bicker with each other.

If you want more ideas like these or better, buy the book *401 Ways to get Your Kids to Work at Home* by Bonnie McCullough and Susan Monson. It is very practical. These ladies are obviously better at getting their kids to work than I am, but I'm probably better at other things.

Outside Help

I hate to even bring up this topic because I know that some of the people reading this book are barely making it on one income. Home schooling is an educational option for many families which could never afford a private education. There are some who have a hard time even coming up with the money for textbooks. I do not want to sow seeds of discontent in any hearts by talking about hiring household help, knowing that it is out of the question for many. There is a saying in Spanish that says, *"No comes pan enfrente los pobres"* which means, "Don't eat bread in front of the poor."

If you know that you are in a situation where household help is out of the question, take a minute to thank the Lord for the things He has given you. Your spouse, your children, the privilege of teaching them, your friends and extended family are all blessings from the hand of a loving Father. The Apostle Paul said,"I have learned that in whatsoever situation I am, therein to be content." Contentment is not dependent on material wealth or external circumstances. I can be content if I am walking in obedience to a God whom I know will supply all my needs according to His riches in glory through Christ Jesus.

The reason I am writing about it is because most people have no idea what is involved. You might be able to get some help and you don't know it. Other authors mention it as a possibility, but give no details. So I am going to talk about it, since it was an answer to prayer for me.

The truth is out . . . Outside help is my secret weapon. I don't know about you, but I have had the idea that only very rich people had household help. The idea had a caste system overtone, with the very upper class hiring the very lowest class (servants) to do their dirty work.

Why is it that a man can hire a secretary to do all the stuff he isn't good at and doesn't have time to do, like spelling and typing, while we women feel guilty if we get help with our housework?

I finally decided that some of the things I was doing could only be done by me, but there were other things that I was doing (or trying to do) that someone else could do. I looked in the Yellow Pages under "Cleaning," and found out that I could get a non-English speaking woman to come for seven hours for only $35.00. (Cost of household help will vary depending on what area you live in, whether the helper speaks English, and how long it has been since I wrote this book in 1987.)

At that particular time it was the windows that were screaming for attention (at one point we had had a nice view). I called the magic number, the lady arrived, and in one day all the windows were sparkling clean. Not only that, but this miracle was wrought *while* I was teaching the kids! The best $35.00 I ever spent. We have seventy-four windowpanes (pains) in our dining room and kitchen alone!

After this, from time to time I would get together some money, swallow my guilt and hire a lady to bail me out. In between times I was still buried in laundry and my house looked like it had been cleaned by a bunch of boys (it had).

At first I tried having someone come in every other week. It helped some, but I still had a hard time holding it all together in between. In fact, I failed miserably. I then tried help once a week; one week she helped with the laundry and the next week with the house. That helped, but we had a lot of kids and a lot of company. I still couldn't keep up in between.

In the meantime I began to see how much I could get done in the other areas of my life when the house was already done. I also saw how nice the house looked when my helper got done, and how pitsy it was by the next afternoon. I realized that it took her seven hours to get it clean and tidy, and twenty-four for us to undo it . . . and half that time we were asleep!

Finally I called an agency to find out how much it would cost to have someone live-in. I found out that in my area a non-English speaking, live-in housekeeper would cost $100.00 per week. This seemed like a lot for us to pay, but room and board in the funny farm is higher, so I began to think about it.

I began to figure. Help with the housework twice a week would be $70.00. For this I got seven hours on two different days. This did not include any money I paid out to baby-sitters or to the kids for doing work around the house. For $30.00 more per week I would have full-time help with the laundry and the house-work, plus baby-sitting five days a week if I needed it. I figured some more. Enrolling my kids in private school would cost at least $670.00 per month, not including school clothes, the hassles of making sack lunches, carpooling, and homework. One reason we started home teaching was because that option was so much less expensive, but we now had plenty of other reasons. My ace in the hole was that I had a home business that generated some income as well as took up large quantities of my time. I talked to my husband and we worked out a deal. He would pay half and I would pay half. It was great for both of us!

I was still worried that I was making a lazy if not foolish choice, but I began praying that if it was the right thing, the Lord would find the right person for me. I told the Lord what I was hoping for:

❑ Someone who didn't mind a house that is full of people all the time.

❑ Someone who didn't mind living without a TV.

❑ Someone with good morals.

❑ A person who wouldn't tease or be unkind to the little ones.

❑ Someone who needed a family like ours.

❑ Someone who would accept my friendship.

The Lord heard and answered! Leticia is an angel straight from Mexico. Not only did she qualify in all the above areas, but she has also come to know Christ since she has come, and is growing in the Lord. God knew the needs of us both and He met them in each other. Since she speaks no English, the kids and my husband are learning some Spanish and I have become quite fluent. This is great practice in language learning which we will need on the mission field soon.

All this to say that God knew my need, and he knows yours too. Please remember that I have a bigger load than most. Many women do fine with help from their kids. Everyone does not need a live-in house-keeper. I have friends who do just fine with help for the heavy cleaning once a month and the everyday stuff is not a problem for them. Others have help with vacuuming, washing floors and ironing once a week. Still others either have older daughters, are very orga-nized by nature, have help, or are comfortable living in happy disarray.

If you decide to hire someone to come at regular intervals to help you out, ask anyone you know who has help where to look. It might be that they know someone who needs a job. If you don't know anyone, I suggest that you look up an agency in the Yellow Pages and find out what is available.

I Have Some Questions . . .

❑ "Who are household workers?" Anyone. There are no stereotypes. In the southwest many Hispanics are employed in homes, but anyone can do it and they come in all types. It could be a student who needs a room in exchange for housework. It could be a neighbor who needs part-time work. It could be someone who lives in with someone else and works for you in her spare time, or someone who is out of work and needs a job.

❑ "What about family privacy?" Most household workers have no interest in family disputes or your personal life. If they don't speak much English, they won't understand much of what is going on anyway. It helps if you have a sep-arate living area for a live-in person so that you all feel some privacy.

❑ "But if I don't speak her language, how will we communicate?" Buy an English/foreign language dictionary right away. Most non-English speakers are eager to learn English and will want to try so that they can keep their jobs. For more money you can hire an English-speaking person if you are concerned about this. Your kids will figure out how to communicate with her very quickly. In fact, it is great language learning experience.

❑ "Won't my children grow up lazy?" Well, they might. This has been our main concern in having a housekeeper. For this reason I still have chores for the kids to do each day. They take the trash out to the alley, clear the table after dinner, feed the animals, and keep the front yard tidy and watered. They aren't allowed to say, "Leticia will clean it up" when they make a mess. They are responsible for their own messes. One advantage I have seen is that they are getting used to living in an orderly house. I hope they will grow up thinking of order as the norm. This was not the case before. Whenever I would start barking orders and begin cleaning like I meant business, the kids would ask, "Who's coming over?"

There is no doubt in my mind that the Proverbs 31 woman had household help. This was not because she was lazy, but rather because she was so industrious. She understood that she could only do so much and needed help to do more.

Whether we get help from our kids, our mothers, or hired help, it is important to remember that it is our job to keep the house livable. We need to *Look well to the ways of our households.* For some of us doing that is more of a struggle than for others, but God knows what he is doing in our lives. Ask, and He will help you to become conformed to the image of Christ in your attitudes and all that you do and say.

6

Mom, Will You Read Us a Story?

There is no frigate like a book
To take us lands away,
Nor any coursers like a page
Of prancing poetry.

This traverse may the poorest take
Without oppress of toll;
How frugal is the chariot
That bears the human soul!
— Emily Dickinson

When I was growing up, we didn't have a TV and my parents read to us a lot. I grew up to be an avid reader and my sisters also read very well. I had always heard that if you read to your children, they would grow up loving books. Experience has borne this out, but it has also been my observation that reading aloud to your children has an even *more* fundamental and far-reaching effect.

We are seeing more and more children who are behind in reading ability. They are coming from both public and private schools. The interesting thing is that many of these kids have *good* phonics backgrounds. They can sound out almost any word you put before them. Their problem is comprehension . . . They read all the words, but still miss what's going on in the story.

Many schools have special groups for these kids in which they do a lot of reading comprehension exercises from workbooks and dittos. The kids are asked to read a paragraph or a short story, then answer questions about the content. The teachers know that if these kids don't learn to understand what they are reading, they will do poorly in all subject areas where reading is involved. If you can't comprehend and retain information from written materials, you will lose out in all subjects.

Let's back away from the problem a little bit and see if we can get another perspective. In the first place, the kids *can* sound out words, so word attack skills are not the problem. Secondly, it appears that it is *groups of words* which pose the problem. In fact, the *larger* the group of words, the *greater* the problem. For example, a child may do well on comprehension dittos, but still be unable to handle a book or a story which involves a number of pages.

The question then is, *"What is it that people who read well do with groups of words that these kids are not able to do?"* The answer is that they convert these groups of words into mental pictures and thus "see" and "hear" what is happening in the story. When I read a story or book, the whole thing happens inside my head. My imagination turns all those groups of words into a wide-screen, living-sound, technicolor production! It is easy for me to remember what happened because I was "there"! Most of us who read well never give a second thought to this process that occurs automatically for us when we read. We just assume it works about the same for everybody.

Why isn't it the same? What keeps some people from developing this "word processing" ability? It is my opinion that it is usually the result of too much TV and/or not being read to enough. Now, please! I am well aware that there are certain kinds of learning problems which produce similar symptoms, but I am not addressing those here. I am writing about this because it is a common problem we are seeing in "normal" kids starting into home schooling in the middle or upper grades. It *is* a problem, but it is *preventable*. It can also be *cured.*

Let's talk about TV first. We all believe that too much TV is bad for kids, and a lot of home schoolers don't even have one. We know that most of the programming doesn't reflect Biblical moral standards, is violent, and promotes materialism and greed. At this point most people who have TVs will mention that there are some good programs on the educational channels. Be that as it may, content is not what we are talking about now. We are considering what is (or is not) happening inside a child's head while he is watching TV.

First of all, when someone is watching TV he is "there" because all the scenery, action, and characterizations come to him through the magic of the screen. There is no need for imagination. In fact, it all happens so fast that there isn't *time* to imagine anything! Such full use is being made of the eye and ear gates that he may hardly taste the sandwich he is eating if there is a lot of action on the screen. Since the story line comes in directly through the primary senses, children have no trouble with TV comprehension. The kids get the story itself, but have no opportunity or need to become involved in creating the details.

When we read, the words on the page represent sights, sounds, smells, and experiences we remember from real life and then bring to our imaginations to become a part of the story we are reading. This takes a certain amount of attentive effort, certainly more than watching it happen on TV.

Another problem with TV when it comes to building reading comprehension skills is that everything takes place in thirty to ninety minutes. This is not only totally unrealistic in terms of the real world, but it requires only a very limited attention commitment to get the whole story. It may take the same time to read a chapter in a book, but that's just a *part* of the story. Reading demands attention and recall over a much longer period of time.

All right, you may say, so what does this have to do with reading aloud? An excellent question! One I was hoping you'd ask!

Often a child with reading problems had his first extended encounter with books and stories when he was learning to read. He was then faced not only with the task of decoding the words, but also with making sense out of *bunches* of words put together. The latter skill is not learned by rote and takes more time to acquire. It really is a *new* skill, since we don't use words quite the same way when we write as we do when we converse. Because of this, the new reader has a problem not only with the words, but with the story (comprehension) as well.

It is a different situation with the child that has been read to. Think for a moment about what happens inside a child's head when he is listening to someone read a story. The words are received through his ears and converted to mental images. He is not processing individual words in this way, but the groups of words that come in a continual flow as the story is read. The reader's inflection and tone of voice help bring out the sense of the words. The imagination creates an unfolding picture, using whatever information the child already has about the things described in the story. The imagination also fills in a myriad of details which could not possibly be covered by the author's narrative.

How many times have you been disappointed when you have seen a movie based on a book you have read? Usually you are disappointed because the movie was not the way you pictured it. You would have cast a completely different type of person for the leading role. The scenery didn't look right. Your imagination had filled in all these things when you read the story. In a movie little is left to the imagination. Certain things are either in the movie or they are not. You come away with the feeling that they left an awful lot out, and they did . . . all the minute details evoked in your own mind by the author's skillful words.

Listening comprehension is essential to reading comprehension. In the school setting, listening comprehension is taught by giving verbal directions. The children are given a group of pictures and instructed to put a circle around the square and color the bird blue. If the child can do this, it is assumed that he can "listen and comprehend." In most kindergarten and first-grade classes, the teacher does read books to the kids. Generally, however, these are books which have more pictures and fewer words; the stories are written in a conversational mode and lack the descriptive imagery and more complex sentence structure found in *real* stories. The class usually discusses what happened in the story, depending heavily on the visual clues from the pictures. This is not enough.

Picture books are fine for the *very* young, but older children need to listen to books that have few visual clues to the story line. The facts of the story should come from the words themselves, and the details should come from the imagination of the child. As the child gets a little older, he should be read stories that cannot be finished in one sitting. A book with chapters, read over a period of time, trains a child to integrate the current episode with what he remembers from the last reading. This helps build long-term memory which, of course, will serve him all his life.

When a child listens to a story the words go in the ears and are converted into mental images. In reading, the exact same process takes place, except that the words enter through the eyes. If a child has been read to, he has already acquired many of the comprehension skills, so all that he needs is to be able to read the words. When he can decode the words themselves, he should be able to comprehend anything he reads which is on his thinking level.

Many mothers choosing to home teach their children were not read to as children. Often the fact that they had trouble in school themselves contributed to their decision to home school. They want to spare their own children the frustration they experienced in school. This is a good idea, but they are frequently quite unaware of all the factors missing in their own education. They may not understand how important it is to read to their children. There is also the problem that many times these mothers do not read well aloud and in fact do not read very well in general. They have only recently begun reading for needed information, like this book, or for spiritual growth, but not for pleasure.

If you fall into this category, there is hope for you and your kids. It is not too late to learn to be a better reader. It is not too late to read to your kids, even if they are older. Even children with little interest in reading themselves generally appreciate being read to. If you are not the greatest reader, take heart . . . You will be helping yourself at the same time you are helping them. Initially it may take some humility on your part as you read aloud to your kids and sometimes stumble over the words. I have a friend who has her kids help her with hard words, and there is a real sense of teamwork and mutual learning.

I would recommend that you read *Honey for a Child's Heart* by Gladys Hunt, and *The Read Aloud Handbook* by Jim Trelease. These will give you helpful tips as well as ideas on what books to choose to read to your children. If you read when you were a child, read the books that you yourself enjoyed. Chose books for them that are on their *thinking* level, not their reading level. For example, your six-year-old may be able to read some Dr. Seuss books, but will thoroughly enjoy hearing *Charlotte's Web* or *Ramona the Pest*, even though he won't be able to read them alone for some time to come. We let our youngest children listen in on stories for the older set, so long as they can sit still and not distract others. It's amazing how much they get out of it and they love the privilege of being included with the big kids. If a story is really good, it can appeal to a wide age span. Children need stories on their own thinking level, but they benefit from being included the other times too.

If you have children in higher grades who have reading problems, I would suggest that you read some older age level books aloud to them, such as *A Wrinkle in Time* by Madeline L'Engle, *The Hobbit* by J. R. R. Tolkien, or *Where the Red Fern Grows* by W. Rawls. It is better if the book is one that they have not seen in movie form. You want them to create the story for themselves, using their imagination.

Read all kinds of stories to your children. Keep a lookout for books with positive messages, desirable character models and good moral values. Read adventures, Bible stories, fantasies, biographies, history, missionary stories, short stories and books from other categories, both fiction and nonfiction. Give them a look at the world! Show them that books can take them anywhere.

Teach subjects like history and science by reading the textbook aloud and discussing it. Have them take turns reading it aloud with you. Have them do the assignments and answer the questions aloud. Often kids who don't read well are auditory learners. This means that they retain what they hear better than what they see or read. By reading and doing the work orally, we combine several means of learning . . . They are reading the words and hearing them at the same time, and then talking about the subject. You will need to do more of the reading for children who haven't yet learned to decode and comprehend at the same time, but their comprehension skills will grow in the process.

If you are really serious about tackling this problem, it would be a good idea to greatly reduce TV watching. None at all would be best. When you read aloud, remove all distractions . . . no music in the background, no paper and pencil to doodle with, and no toys. You are giving this activity your full attention and it deserves theirs. In the evenings when Dad reads, we like to dim the lights and get cozy . . . maybe light a fire in the fireplace. Anything which makes the time special adds to the pleasure associated with reading. If a child has never learned to imagine from a story made of words, he will really need to give it his undivided attention. Put yourself into it and read with expression; the kids love it! All skills improve with practice, and the more you read aloud, the better you will do it.

If you really want to see your child become a *reader*, I would also suggest that you require forty-five minutes to an hour of independent reading per day for the fairly good readers, eight years or older. This is a time during which they may read a book of their choice and they may do nothing else. I find that a good time for this is after lunch. If the child can't find a book within a reasonable amount of time, I find one for him. I try to pick one I think he will like, but if after a few chapters he still doesn't like it and can give me an intelligent reason why, I let him choose another.

At first it may be a good idea to give a reward for each book read. This way they can't help but win a prize. Since they must read every day, eventually they *will* finish a book! I've given my younger kids a dollar for their first "real" book and a quarter for each of the next twenty-five books. Mine have never been reluctant readers, so I don't have to go to extreme measures. The reluctant ones may need more incentives, however, and I believe it is worth whatever it takes to get them reading.

I do not recommend book reports unless you have a child who loves to write them. For many kids who have been in school, the only time they read a book was because they had to produce one of those odious book reports. This is the only way a teacher can keep track of who's reading in a class of thirty. How many book reports have you written as an adult? It is a better idea to read the same book that your child is reading, and then talk about it together. How nice to share books as "mutual friends" with your child. You want to foster the idea that books bring pleasure, not pain.

To sum up, reading is very important! You need to encourage it at every point. Read aloud to your children a lot! In our house there have been days when we began reading at 9 in the morning and didn't stop until noon because we just couldn't stand to put the book down. This is not skipping school; it is just a different type of school day. Next make it your goal to get your kids reading for themselves. You will never regret it and they will always be grateful to you for it.

7

A School
and Her Money
Are Soon Parted

*The writing of many books is
endless,
and excessive devotion to books
is wearying to the body.*
— Ecclesiastes 12:12

hen you begin to look into the nuts and
bolts of home schooling, you find that
your decision to home school was only
the beginning of many difficult choices.
You are now a consumer in a whole new field. It seems
that every home school group, book company, toy
company, home business and educational expert has
"just the thing you need to do right by your child."

You are a sitting duck for educational suppliers.
Beware! It is not that these products are no good . . .
Quite the contrary, they *all* have merit. It is just that
without a plan, you will buy and buy and buy and still
feel that you don't have it covered. Unless you have a
teaching background or are very confident and creative,
you will feel insecure about pulling a curriculum out of
the air. How will you know what to cover and to what
depth to cover it? What if the children don't understand

it? How can you hit the subject from another angle? How much should you expect each child to do in a day's work? You need answers to these questions.

What usually happens is that when a problem arises, we tend to throw money at it. Buy another workbook, buy a game that teaches it, or buy a computer and a bunch of educational software. Not only is this expensive, usually more so than a complete curriculum, but you also have a problem with continuity. Most subjects are best taught "line upon line, precept upon precept." Changing approaches several times during the year may end up confusing your child. This is especially true if you don't really know in what order to present the skills necessary for proficiency. In math and phonics, for example, the sequence of skills taught is crucial.

It is my advice, especially if it is your first year, or if the last paragraph describes your experience, that you find a good, complete curriculum and stick with it for one year. Flex within that program, but don't buy *anything* else. After this, you will be in a good position to judge what you want to do differently next time. It may be that you will be ready for the eclectic approach, or that you will want to stay with what you've been using, or try a different program. During the first year you will have the chance to meet other home schooling mothers and go to workshops and conferences. You will become aware of, and at times confused by, all that is available. But please, unless you know for sure that what you are using is a loser, don't change horses in midstream.

When you look at a program, here are some things to consider before you buy.

Approach

Try to understand the characteristics of each curriculum and be realistic about the time required to prepare lessons. The more kids you have, the less time you have.

First there are the unit study programs. *KONOS* is a multi-level one based on Christian character qualities. *The Weaver* is built on the Bible, beginning in Genesis. *The Principle Approach* teaches everything on the basis of certain Biblical principles; all subjects are presented within the framework of the main theme (or unit) of the program. These unit studies programs are full of wonderful ideas and projects, and are a lot of fun because learning isn't compartmentalized into "subjects," and each day is a new adventure.

These programs *appear* to be timesavers because they are multi-level and can be used with all of your kids at once. The hitch is that some of us aren't up to an adventure every day, and unit studies programs often require a great deal of preparation. Someone must go to the library and round up the needed resource books; you must have on hand all the necessary equipment for any projects in the unit. If you are the type of person who revels in research and is thrilled with the idea of synthesizing many elements into one Scripture-oriented program, this is the type of curriculum for you. One other thing to remember is that these programs usually don't include math and phonics, so you will need to buy something else to cover these.

On the other hand, we have the "programmed learning" type of curriculum, (A.C.E., Basic Education, Alpha Omega, and Christian Light). In these programs the child works in workbooks all the time and the mother has virtually no preparation to do and minimal teaching. She must be there to answer questions and to correct the work. This is not a bad approach if the child is reading well and needs an environment with achievable goals. This is also a good option for parents who are not well-educated themselves, or who were educated in another country and therefore feel that they cannot adequately teach subjects such as American history or English grammar. It is a timesaver for the mom who must work outside the home, or who has just had twins. I have used Alpha Omega for science with my older boys with satisfactory results. I can't keep track of this subject very well otherwise.

This type of program is not without its drawbacks, however. Since, in order to learn this way, one must read and comprehend large amounts of written material, a student without good reading skills will do poorly and will tend to feel frustrated and overwhelmed. It is inadvisable to use this approach with an auditory learner. Even for good readers, some of these programs have the disadvantage that most of the learning is by rote; the lessons rely on short-term rather than long term memory.

Programmed learning material is presented in short paragraphs, followed by questions requiring short answers. This continues until the self-test is reached. All facts are reviewed by the student and he then takes the test. There are several self-tests in the booklet and then a final exam. A passing grade is 80 percent or better. The whole booklet is to be done in about a month. Think for a minute. How many of the dates you had to memorize in junior high history do you still remember? Probably none, since you learned it for the test and not for your own interest.

Often there is not a sense of continuity in a subject area since each booklet more or less stands alone. The student may know a lot of facts but be missing the whole picture of how all the facts fit together. This overall picture is needed in science, history, and Bible.

Some workbooks stimulate very little creative or original thought. There is little call for the student to analyze and observe the philosophy or writing style of different authors. Even kids who do well often get bored, since the format is always the same. It is important to add creative writing, discussion and independent reading to programs of this type. I believe this kind of format lends itself best to filling in holes in an otherwise complete curriculum.

Of the three curriculums mentioned above, I would recommend Alpha Omega over the others. They have some very helpful materials for home schoolers, and encourage the parent to really teach, not just supervise.

They have tried to bring more inductive reasoning into their question-and-answer format, although much of it is still geared to short term memory.

A systematic review of the records of all 1984-85 Bob Jones University students graduating from both public and Christian high schools shows that these workbook-centered programs have some weaknesses in the math area. This university has had to provide special remedial classes for most of the students coming from schools using this approach before they can handle college-level work. We have found that the kids in these types of curriculum do fairly well in math computation, but have lower than expected scores in math concepts and problem-solving on standardized tests. If your child is college-bound, think twice about using this kind of program exclusively for very long.

Philosophy of Life

Another important thing to look for in choosing a curriculum is philosophy and frame of reference.

For example, Rod and Staff curriculum is written from an Anabaptist philosophy and a small-town frame of reference. Due to the mindset of the authors, the illustrations are black and white and all the women in the books will be wearing "plain clothes" and head-coverings. History will be taught from a philosophy of pacifism and nonparticipation in government. They believe that children should not be evangelized, but rather taught about the Bible and the Christian life and left to make a decision when they reach the age of accountability. The small-town frame of reference results in most of the story settings being in small farming communities rather than big cities. There are few if any blacks, Hispanics, or orientals in the texts. Since all the readers are vocabulary-controlled Bible stories, there is no room for imaginative stories in the lower grades. Their theme is "A good education is the result of diligence and hard work," and they really work the kids with rote and drill.

A contrasting example is Bob Jones University Press. They believe that fundamental Biblical truth applies to every aspect of a Christian's life and should be taught in every subject at every level, but in a clear and natural way. These books teach that Christians should serve and support their country, and that children can not only be born again, but that they should lead their friends to Christ. Their frame of reference is that of universal appeal (city/country, different races, different countries, fiction/nonfiction, past and present), and academic excellence through understanding.

Before you buy a curriculum, it is a good idea to find out what the authors are teaching in addition to academic subjects. Just as we need to monitor secular textbooks for humanism, we need to be aware of doctrine in Christian textbooks. With all of the textbooks available, why did these people decide to write another one? If you are to be happy with a curriculum, you must agree with the philosophy of the authors, and with their frame of reference.

Textbooks

There is a great deal of discussion about using classroom curriculum in a home school setting. "Remember," we are told, "home school isn't just a school in a home." What is implied is that if we use materials that are used in classrooms we aren't really home schooling, somehow. I agree that a home school that has buzzers marking recesses and class breaks, with all the kids lining up behind Mom and marching to the backyard, is a little absurd. I also feel that working in total silence and raising hands for questions in a three-kid classroom is unnecessary. So is doing every subject every day and having class every day until 3:00 P.M. I don't understand, however, how having a hodge-podge curriculum made up of a little of this and a little of that, or using books that are over eighty years old, is somehow more "home school" than a well laid out program.

A mother called me the other day. She had been home schooling for two years, but was frustrated and feeling like a failure. She was so discouraged that she ended up having school about twice a week. I asked her what she was using for curriculum. She said that she was using a set of rewritten antique readers (which her daughter read well, but did not enjoy), a math game, and spelling and English books that she liked from a mainline curriculum. For history she had purchased a fairly expensive set of biographies. She was totally dismayed to find that many of them were so poorly written that even *she* couldn't stand to read them, and it was worse with the kids! This set of books was to have been her whole history program for several years. No wonder she was discouraged! She said that every time she tried to find out what other people were doing they told her that she shouldn't compare, but just figure out what *her* kids needed, based on her knowledge of them. Sigh . . . now what?

Why had she gone this route? Because it was recommended by authorities as "not too structured." It was not very expensive either, and no one gave her any other ideas. For her, it was not structured enough, caused her to spend a lot of extra money filling in the holes with workbooks which didn't hang together and a lot of extra time trying to figure out what to do next .

I suggested that she buy the rest of the material that went with the spelling and English that she already liked, and scrap the other. She did, and she and her daughter both love it. Now every day she knows exactly what she will be covering and how. From her teacher's manual she can pick and choose what reinforcement activities to use, if any. Her assignments are purposeful and reasonable in length.

Am I saying then that curriculum geared to the classroom can be used in the home with no problem at all? No, there can be problems. Some programs are more easily adapted than others. We need to maintain a balance. We need to build a child's knowledge from the foundation up in an orderly manner, and yet do it at a pace that matches the child's abilities and interest. Good textbooks give us order and direction and stimulate interest, but we need to use wisdom as to how much or little time we spend on a given concept. The object is not to finish the books by June 5th. Our goal should be to teach the child what he needs to know, and not move on until he is proficient. There is no point in teaching division if a child doesn't know his multiplication facts. On the other hand, there is no point in doing ten pages of multiplication drills just because they're in the book if he already knows them well. Perhaps five review problems a day would suffice to keep him from getting rusty.

Often a textbook designed to be taught by a teacher is taught poorly by a mother because she doesn't use the teacher's manual. Teacher's manuals often offer alternate approaches to presenting a concept that a child missed on the first pass. Enrichment and hands-on activities are suggested which you may wish to use, if the child is interested and you have the time. Often these are great ideas we would never think of on our own, yet they are very simple to implement. Discussion and other oral activities, such as mental math, are included that are not in the child's textbook. Directions are given for many simple learning games that kids love.

It is important to remember when you are using a teacher's manual that some suggested activities are only suitable for groups of children. Just skip these. Other activities can be adapted. When the teacher's manual calls for word flash cards, I write the words on a piece of paper in list form. This saves a lot of time. Even among the appropriate and valuable activities, methods, and projects suggested, you will want to pick and choose the ones best suited to you and your child. There just isn't time or the need to do them all. The point is that you have access to many creative ideas that tie right in with what you are teaching, but are not dependent on your own inspiration. This means that you can do well even on a bad day.

Christian Textbooks

The two biggest publishers of textbooks for Christian schools are A Beka Books and Bob Jones University Press.

A Beka materials came out at a time when there was a tremendous need for a Christian alternative to secular textbooks. Their goal was to produce a curriculum with high academic standards and a Christian perspective. In a very short time, they pulled together a complete program which has been and continues to be used in many Christian schools.

If you are considering the A Beka program, it is important to realize that A Beka stresses *accelerated* learning on all levels. It is my understanding that third-grade secular math books were adapted and made into the second-grade texts, and so on down the line. The same was done for the readers. Home schoolers using this curriculum will want to consider this as they choose the right level book for the child, and move at a pace appropriate for the child being taught, rather than at the classroom pace recommended in the teacher's manuals. This program includes a lot of drill and practice, so there is a lot of busywork that the home schooler may want to eliminate. The developers want their kindergarten students to be reading by Christmas. As a result, there is a lot of pressure on these little guys. Children in lower grades are also made to do a lot of writing practice, which most home schoolers do not feel is appropriate for five- and six-year-olds.

A bright child will probably perform very well with this program. He will learn facts, be able to state principles, and master skills at an early age. There is some question as to whether his maturity level will enable him to understand these facts and apply these principles in other contexts. Skills are mastered primarily through rote memorization and drill, rather than through comprehension and application. It is the difference between memorizing the parts of a flower and taking several flowers apart to compare them.

❏ 59

This program is not only geared to classroom use—it is produced with classroom management in mind. For example, hands-on activities usually produce a better understanding of a concept than memorization and drill, but it is more difficult for a teacher to maintain order among thirty kids tearing up flowers than thirty children sitting quietly at their desks memorizing flower parts. In a classroom, bright students finish their work early and need something to keep them busy . . . so busywork is provided in the curriculum. Students who are having trouble may need extra drill . . . so the same busywork solution is called in.

If the recommended pace is followed, these kids will spend hours in their books and become good studiers. Some kids in Christian schools using this program cannot take the pressure and burn out, becoming academic casualties.

A number of home schoolers enjoy using A Beka textbooks without the teacher's guides and busywork. Many of these books are well written and provide a good Christian slant on history and science. Their literature books have good stories in them, and I believe they are all written by Christian authors in the upper grades.

A Beka has only recently been willing to sell to home schoolers at the retail price. Although you pay for the teacher's manuals, they remain the property of A Beka and may not be sold or passed along.

A Beka also has a video school that they recommend for home school families also. The child watches a classroom teacher from Pensacola Christian Academy on TV and does his work with that class. I would not recommend doing all of school this way, but it might be helpful to do one subject, like eighth grade science, for variety and to give you a break. I think right now it costs about $650.00 for all junior high classes.

Bob Jones University Press is a relative newcomer to the Christian textbook scene. Not being satisfied with what was available for their own Christian schools, they decided to write their own curriculum, from the bottom up. This program has been about ten years in development and will be complete, K through 12, in 1988.

Some are a little concerned about using curriculum from Bob Jones University because of their judgmental attitude towards the rest of the Christian community. I was very leery myself. I didn't want my kids to come out like "those guys." The books looked so good, however, that I decided to try a few. I can unabashedly say that I was won over.

In using Bob Jones University books over the last four years I have seen nothing of a judgmental, legalistic attitude. You may notice that all the women wear dresses, but no mention is made of it. There are people of all races in the books, but you will not see mixed racial couples. Once again, they don't draw attention to this fact. I have yet to find anything objectionable, and in fact I feel that Christianity is presented in a very positive and natural way.

The same perfectionist standard that the Bob Jones people demand of everyone else they also demand of themselves and this has produced, in my opinion, the best books on the market.

The educational philosophy of Bob Jones University Press is that children need to understand what they are learning. "Knowledge is easy to him that has understanding."

The goal of the program is to produce Christians who can think, not merely perform. Much time is spent in teaching the interrelationship between facts and application of principles. The methods used stress problem-solving, inductive reasoning, reading comprehension, and learning through hands-on activities. Kids are not pushed to learn skills they are not ready for or that they don't understand. There is very little busywork. Drill activities are short and designed to build and reinforce concepts that are already understood by the child.

The Beginnings Program for kindergarten and first grade is great! It starts out very slowly (six weeks to learn the names of the letters) and is fun for the child. It uses songs, finger plays, rhymes, poems and fairy tales to teach basic concepts. The idea is to give the kids a good foundation and a positive attitude toward learning right from the start. There is very little writing in kindergarten. Children trace the letters four times and do it once on their own. Later they may write two- or three-word sentences. You can skip these writing activities if you prefer. The teaching is done aloud using big fat teacher's manuals. These manuals do everything except tell you when to inhale and exhale, which is wonderful if you haven't the foggiest idea how to teach a child to read.

I find that the BJU teacher's manuals are a great help. Without them I tend to expect way too much of my kids in each subject. They are very realistic in their expectations of the kids, which I still need even after doing this for five years.

The BJU textbook people feel that for a textbook to be Christian in the full extent of the word, it must qualify on many levels. It should, first of all, be consistent with Biblical revelation in its presentation of facts in each subject area. Biblical priorities and character should be taught and illustrated in every subject. A neat example of this is in the Bob Jones Heritage Studies program. Why does a Christian need to know about people who live in other parts of the world? In order to fulfill the Great Commission of Christ; to go into the world and preach the gospel. In these textbooks, people from other lands, their language and culture are presented along with their need for Christ. The children are challenged to consider going to a people who have never heard the gospel as missionaries when they grow up.

Secondly, Bob Jones University Press believes that Christians should learn discernment. Our children will encounter many conflicting messages out there in the big world someday. They need to understand how to evaluate what they are hearing. In the upper grades, non-Christian scientists, historians and authors are presented along with their theories or philosophies. The students are taught to see where these ideas came from, what they mean and what the end-results of that kind of thinking will be. Then we are taken to Scripture to see what God says about the subject; we see the results of godliness or wickedness, truth or error in these areas. Kids must be taught to think, compare, reason, and discern. They need to see how "this" fits together with "that" and draw a conclusion.

The people at BJU Press have adopted home schoolers like family members. They have a toll free line that anyone may call, not just for ordering, but to get help. The number is: (800) 845-5731. I have a friend who had a question about teaching math and talked for fifteen minutes with the author of the algebra text. I haven't heard of anyone yet who has encountered anyone on the phone who was grumpy or in a hurry. They sell to home schoolers at the wholesale price and usually ship the same day, if it is not the rush season (between May and August). You can order by mail or by phone, pay C.O.D., VISA or Mastercard.

BJU has put on teacher workshops for home schoolers that are very practical, and publish a quarterly newsletter called *The Home School Helper.* These people really believe that parents can and should be able to do a good job teaching their own kids.

Secular Textbooks

This may sound like heresy, but a good secular textbook is better than a lousy "Christian" textbook. Truth is truth, no matter who says it, and poor teaching is still poor, even when sprinkled with Bible verses.

What is a secular textbook? It is a book written, usually by non-Christians, for the purpose of teaching academic subjects. Some of these books, such as those offered through the Calvert Correspondence Course, do an exceptional job of teaching. The Open Court Rise program is excellent for advanced fourth through sixth grade language and reading, and their

Real Math is also a very good series. The John Saxon math program is probably the best one on the market; we highly recommend it and it is secular. I have a favorite junior high English text that is secular (McDougal Littel, *Building English Skills*). I like it because it clearly teaches good writing skills step by step.

Secular textbooks vary widely in their presentation of secular values, and the older they are, the less likely they are to be offensive. *The Golden Rule Reading Series*, published in the 1950s by the State of California, is full of wonderful character-building stories and some of these stories are from the Bible. These are the books that were reprinted by A Beka for their reading program. Care needs to be taken, however, with math books written in the Sixties and Seventies because "new math" was being pushed at that time, and proved to be a failure.

If you are using a secular textbook, you should pre-read everything your children are reading. This is especially true for the more subjective areas such as reading, social studies and science, and more so if the books were published after 1975. Even in math books, word problems may emphasize women in non-traditional roles and other off-the-wall propaganda that you wouldn't expect to find in a math book. These objectionable items do not necessarily mean you should toss the book. They can be the basis for some lively discussion.

A well-educated Christian child should at some point be exposed to how the world thinks. This is best done in a controlled situation, such as a home school. The parent needs to bring this kind of thinking into the light of Scripture, and expose it as a lie. If you are not willing to go to this extra work, or do not know how to recognize humanistic teaching, do not use secular textbooks. Even if they are free, they are not worth it.

Cost

Ah! There's the rub. Everything costs money. First let me say something about planning ahead. If you are thinking about home teaching, you know you will need some curriculum. Please start saving now. I can't believe how many people call me who have been thinking about or planning to home school for quite some time and yet are unprepared to spend any money. Each year you will need to buy some new things, so each year you should set aside some money so it will be there when the time comes to buy books.

Choose your curriculum carefully. We have already covered the most important factors to keep in mind. If you can at all help it, don't let cost be your primary criterion in textbook choice. If you get a great deal on what you want, fantastic! But good curriculum is worth saving for. As my husband says, "If you think education is expensive, you should try ignorance." The same can be said for inadequate curriculum.

If you have a large family, it is important to also consider whether your chosen curriculum is of the quality that will hold up to long use. Workbooks must be purchased each year for each grade. The initial cost is low, but over a three- or four-year period you will spend over twice as much on workbooks as on a hardbound program. Paperbound texts don't hold up well over the long haul, but hardbound books do. Since I have seven kids, I already have most of what I need in hardbound books, and therefore I don't spend that much anymore.

In our home school organization, many of us are using the same types of curriculum. This is great because we can sell what we no longer need and buy what we now need, used. We make up a list with everything that anyone wants to sell with each person's phone number. This is circulated and people can then wheel and deal on their own.

Guidelines for Selecting Curriculum

❑ Curriculum is built from any item that helps you teach a subject. This includes things like dominos and coins for math, or a globe for social studies.

❑ Not all curriculum needs to be bought and paid for. Library books can be used for science, social studies, and literature, and you can share books with other home schoolers.

❑ Most families buy more curriculum than they need. The fear of not doing a good job can contribute to impulse spending.

❑ Don't buy anything sight unseen, no matter who says it's wonderful. Look at someone else's, call the sales representative, wait 'til a book fair. Check it out.

❑ Don't buy anything that doesn't appeal to you personally. If you don't like it, you won't use it. This is true even if you think the child needs it or that *he* would like it.

❑ Keep in mind your own personality when considering a purchase. Do you like research and intricate projects that require prior preparation time? Then you might enjoy the unit-study method used in KONOS, Weaver, or the Principle Approach. If you like everything already organized and spelled out, you should go for a traditional textbook and teacher's manual.

❑ Keep in mind the personality of your child. Would he feel a sense of accomplishment upon completing a workbook? Or is it like pulling teeth to get him to write his name on a paper? This child would do better with hands-on materials and oral work.

❑ Buy only for your present needs. Your enthusiasm for using an item is highest at the time of purchase. You could push a child past his capabilities in your desire to use the item, or you may have changed your approach by the time you get to it and it doesn't fit. My cupboards are full of such items!

❑ If you don't like a subject (e.g., math), ask the Lord to increase your interest and ability. Your attitude will be reflected in your kids. I have learned math right along with my kids. Since it is hard for me, I feel I am better able to help my kids when it is hard for them. If they see me learning, they will learn too, and realize that people can learn all their lives.

❑ Buy foundational materials (readin', 'ritin', and 'rithmetic) first.

❑ Before going to a curriculum fair or teacher's supply store, decide exactly what you intend to buy. This will help keep you from impulse buying and from being overwhelmed by all the possibilities.

❑ Plan to buy items throughout the year: Christmas, birthdays, or when enthusiasm is flagging.

❑ Arrange swaps or buy used materials from other home schoolers.

❑ Remember: Teachers teach, books don't. An item is only as valuable as the amount of use it receives. The actual amount of learning that takes place depends on you and your child.

Many good seminars and workshops are geared to home schooling parents. Go to them! Take notes, hear new ideas and meet people. It may be that what you are doing is not what the speaker said, but it is working well for you. When you get home, think about what you have been doing, figure out if you need to make changes. If so, *make a plan to implement these changes* and give it your best shot. Let these workshops be an encouragement rather than a guilt trip. Remember too, if you have a good complete curriculum you probably don't need what they are selling. I speak from experience! I don't like to think how many hundreds of dollars worth of stuff I have here that we never even look at. It was all too good to pass up, but it's no good at all if you don't use it.

In all of this it is important to keep in mind your goals of teaching the "whole" child. Remember that your best teaching tool is your life. We need to be examples of diligence, patience, long-suffering, joy, peace and a sense of humor. After all, Rome wasn't built in a day.

This book is not meant to be an extensive curriculum guide. For more information about curriculum and ordering—including the addresses and prices of most programs mentioned in this chapter—read Mary Pride's *NEW Big Book of Home Learning* and her *Next Book of Home Learning* (available in Christian bookstores). In addition to excellent reviews on a multitude of textbooks and other learning materials, each is fun to read and full of "right-on" discussions on a variety of home school-related topics.

Our own home school organization, Painter Avenue Christian School, has developed a recommended curriculum. We have found that first-timers usually need to start with a good program suggested by someone else. Then, the next year, they at least know what they don't like and can make a more educated choice for the following year.

Recommended Curriculum for
Painter Avenue Christian School

These recommendations are subject to change as the selection available to home schoolers broadens and as we become familiar with more products.

Kindergarten: Lots of play and reading aloud
Math: Count things and answer their questions
Grandma's Garden Felt Math
Bob Jones *Beginnings Program ABC* or Play 'N Talk

First Grade: Lots of reading aloud
Language Arts: Bob Jones *Beginnings Program DEF*
Math: Bob Jones first-grade math

Second Grade: Lots of reading aloud
Language Arts: BJU Writing and Grammar, Reading, Spelling
Math: BJU, level 2
Social Studies (if you want): BJU Heritage Studies or A Beka

Third Grade: Lots of reading aloud
Language Arts: BJU Writing and Grammar, Reading, Spelling
Math: Modern Curriculum Press Mathematics, level C (work-text) or BJU math, level 3 (hardbound)
Social Studies: BJU Heritage Studies (fantastic)
Science (if you want): BJU

Fourth Grade: Independent reading
Language Arts: BJU Writing and Grammar, Reading, Spelling or Open Court Rise Program*

Math: *Elementary Mathematics* level 4,** by Stephen D. Hake or BJU math, level 4
Social Studies: BJU Heritage Studies (great)
Science: BJU

Fifth Grade: Independent Reading
Language Arts: BJU Writing and Grammar, Reading, Spelling or Open Court Rise Program*
Math: *Math 65,* by Saxon and Hake or BJU math, level 5
Social Studies: BJU Heritage Studies (wonderful)
Science: BJU

Sixth Grade: Independent Reading
Language Arts: BJU Writing and Grammar, Reading, Spelling or Open Court Rise Program*
Math: *Math 76,* by Saxon and Hake or BJU math, level 6
Social Studies: BJU Heritage Studies (superb)
Science: BJU

Seventh Grade: Independent Reading
English: *Building English Skills,* red level; McDougal Littel; or BJU if you have used previous levels
Literature: BJU, level 7
Math: *Math 76,* by Saxon and Hake or BJU math, level 7
Social Studies: BJU *World Studies* (magnificent)
Science: BJU *Life Science* (in-depth) or Alpha Omega (sufficient)

Eighth Grade: Independent reading
English: *Building English Skills*,
green level; McDougal Littel;
or BJU if you have used
previous levels
Literature: BJU level 8
Math: *Algebra 1/2*, by John
Saxon or BJU math, level 8
Social Studies: *America, Her
People and Values* (Harcourt,
Brace and Jovonavich) or
BJU American History, avail-
able 1989
Science: BJU *Earth Science* (in-
depth) or Alpha Omega (suf-
ficient)

Ninth Grade: Independent reading
English: *Building English Skills*,
orange level; McDougal
Littel; or BJU if you have
used previous levels
Literature: BJU level 9, Modern
American Literature
Math: *Algebra 1*, John Saxon; or
BJU Consumer Math (if
needed)
Social Studies: BJU *Geography*
(excellent)
Science: BJU *Basic Science*
(heavy duty) or Alpha Omega
(Biology)

---

* Open Court is not a complete language arts program
unless you use the teacher's manuals.
** Write to Stephen D. Hake, 10662 Lora, Temple City,
CA 91780

High School Recommendations

At this point, so much depends on why your child is not enrolled in a conventional school, that it is very difficult to make general recommendations.

Independent reading is important on all levels. By this time, most kids either enjoy reading or avoid it at all costs. In either case, it is a good idea to give them a reading list from which to pick books, so that you have some say as to what they do read. Read the same books they do and talk about them. If necessary, read aloud together and/or require regular periods of independent reading.

English: By now your teenager should be able to express himself well in writing. He should be able to describe, explain, defend, inform and correspond. He should be able to use and understand a large vocabulary, spell correctly (or use a dictionary), punctuate, capitalize and use proper grammar. If he can't, you have your work cut out for you and you should consider using a lower (seventh or eighth) grade curriculum in this area. If he is able to write well, enroll him in the local junior college English course, or regularly require writing assignments relating to his other subject areas.

Literature: see Independent Reading. BJU literature books on the high school level are great. They expose students to many world-renowned authors, secular as well as Christian, and teach analysis and discernment as well as literary style.

Math: If the student is performing at grade level, he already has all of the basic math skills he needs. If he is performing below grade level, a remedial course emphasizing practical, everyday uses of mathematics is in order, and he should become adept with a calculator. If the student is interested and bright in this area, or planning to pursue a career that requires a strong math background he should continue with the typical college prep program of algebra, geometry, etc. It is wise for your child to get as much math under his belt as is reasonable, because quitting too soon will limit his possibilities for the future.

Social Studies: BJU continues to provide an excellent program in this area. If the child is a poor reader, this subject could be handled by a lower level textbook or by Mom reading aloud. Remember, if your child does not have the 3 R's down by now, emphasize them over social studies.

Science: BJU's program is outstanding for the student who has interest and ability in this area. Excellent college prep material. However, it is pretty overwhelming for average high schoolers. For these, Alpha Omega is a possibility, or science classes at a junior college (but these courses make no provision for the non-diligent). Once again, science is of low priority for the kid who does not have his basics down. If covered at all, it should be taught with materials at the child's reading level or by projects and read aloud with Mom.

Miscellaneous: If he does not already have these skills, your high-schooler should learn to type (try the local junior college) and to administer first aid (maybe through a community service program).

Further Comment on Using the Local Junior College

These colleges are hotbeds of secular humanism. It is often the goal of the teachers to make major changes in the thinking of their students at this crucial time in their lives. I highly recommend having your child read and discuss with you (you read it too!) the book *How to Be Your Own Selfish Pig* by Susan Schaffer Macaulay *before* they attend their first class. This book covers the current philosophies believed and taught in our world and brings them clearly into the light of Scripture. Then keep up with what is happening in your child's classes and talk about what is being taught.

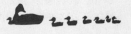

8

Testing . . . 1-2-3

For God sees not as man sees,
for man looks at the outward
appearance,
but the Lord looks at the heart.
— 1 Samuel 16:7

M ost home schooling mothers view achievement testing with a certain degree of nervousness. This is completely normal and understandable. After all, I am being tested just as certainly as my child is. What if he didn't learn anything I tried to teach him? What if we didn't cover everything we should have? Have I taken on a job I'm not really qualified for . . . and blown it? Am I ready for the *awful truth?* Hopefully in this chapter we will relieve some anxiety and dispel some myths.

Why Should Our Kids Be Tested?

In the first place, most of us are curious to know how it is *really* going! The achievement test results will provide an unbiased evaluation of our child's progress in basic subject areas. We want to know if he is where he should be, and look forward to receiving information about his strengths and weaknesses. Usually we have found that the test scores confirm what the mother had already thought about her child's performance.

The test may point out weaknesses in your curriculum or teaching, enabling you to adjust your style, provide supplemental or remedial work, and in general keep you on the right track.

Testing your child shows those standing around watching you that you are not afraid of an objective analysis. You are not trying to hide anything from yourself or them. Many fathers who were quite unsure about home schooling felt much better after seeing some solid test scores. Grandparents are also reassured by numbers. So are some school authorities.

Who Should Be Tested?

As a general rule, we recommend yearly testing for children who are able to read. Usually, it is better not to test first-graders. Most home schoolers move at a relaxed pace with their young children, and they are not ready to perform well at these early stages . . . especially if you are following the "wait until eight" approach.

If you have an older child (age ten or more), and you have been unable to make much progress academically with him, some diagnostic testing may be in order. This is different than academic achievement testing. See Chapter 10 for more information.

How Should They Be Tested?

The best place for testing seems to be the same environment in which the child is schooled: in his own home, by his own mother. A test administered by a stranger in an unfamiliar place will not be as accurate because of the stress involved.

Professionals usually frown on a test administered by nonprofessionals. Mere mothers do not have the "necessary special training" to administer such tests properly. However, as a certified teacher in the public schools, I administered standardized tests with *no* training whatsoever. The instructions are quite complete . . . They practically tell you when to inhale and exhale.

The most common procedure is to read the instructions aloud to the child exactly as they are written. You give him the practice questions provided to make sure he understands what to do. Then you set the timer and leave him alone to work. Your sole responsibility now is to make sure he does not cheat and is not unduly disturbed, and to stop him when his time is up.

A perhaps more valid objection to mother-administered tests is the fact that the mother is not a neutral party. As the child's parent and teacher she has a lot at stake in his performance, and might be tempted to help him. But why would you want to do that? As a mother, you more than anyone should want an accurate measurement of your child's achievement (and your own). Be sure you do follow the proper procedures. Don't explain what questions mean or help him with words he does not know.

If you are the one who wants the test results, there should be no problem with doing the testing yourself. However, if some official (as under a court order) wants an evaluation, find a credentialed teacher to administer the test.

We recommend that you intersperse math tests with the other ones so that the kids don't get burned out on one subject. The testing should be done when the child is well rested, usually in the morning. Choose a day when he is not anticipating or dreading something in the afternoon, like Disneyland or a tonsillectomy. He should not eat junk food for breakfast. Do the testing for a couple of hours a day (about the same period of time you would normally conduct school) and allow a short break every hour or so. This will spread most tests over two or three days.

How Do I Read Test Scores?

Most achievement test results are given in raw scores, grade equivalent scores and percentile scores.

RAW SCORE. A raw score basically just tells how many questions the child answered correctly. It does not help much in determining how well the child did. It is to the rest of the scores what a raw chicken is to chicken soup.

GRADE EQUIVALENT SCORE. The grade-equivalent score is given in a decimal format. For example, a score of 5.7 means that your child performed at a level of fifth grade in the seventh month. This means that your child did as well on this test as an average child in the seventh month of fifth grade would do on *this* level of the test.

Suppose your second-grader scores 5.7 in math. It does not mean that your child is working at a fifth-grade, seventh-month level. If he had taken the fifth-grade test, he most likely would not have scored at this level. You should not assume that he already knows all that he needs to know to be a fifth-grader. As his teacher you know that there is a lot of information between second and fifth grade that he doesn't know. He should not immediately be jumped from second- to fifth- grade curriculum. However, this high score may indicate that this is a strong area for him, and perhaps you can move more rapidly through the material. Maybe you can even skip certain concepts that you know he understands well. Avoiding busywork is one of the advantages of home schooling

Suppose your eighth-grader scored 5.7 in math. The seventh month is almost the end of fifth grade. Knowing that math books generally start out with a hefty review of the previous year's work, I would recommend a sixth grade level book for this child. Move slowly enough to catch the trouble spots. If your child would be embarrassed to be working in a book with a big "6" on the front of it, look for a curriculum that is more subtly marked. For example, *Math 76* by John Saxon would be ideal.

PERCENTILE SCORE. A percentile score compares your child to other children in his grade level. A percen*tile* score is not to be confused with the percen*tage* of questions answered correctly. A percentage score of 67 means that for every hundred questions, sixty-seven were answered correctly. A percentile score of 67 means that out of one hundred children in the same grade who took this test, this child scored better than sixty-seven of them. A percentile score of 50 means that the child is right in the middle. Fifty scored below him, he was number 51, and forty-nine scored above him. The highest possible percentile score is 99. Out of one hundred children, ninety-nine scored lower than this child.

How Do Home-Taught Children Perform on Achievement Tests?

In our experience, home-taught children tend to score well above the 50th percentile. By the very nature of percentile, in an average group half of the children would score below 50 and half at or above 50. As a group, therefore, home-taught children seem to do better than average.

There are two possible explanations for this. One is that we are right in our belief that a smaller student to teacher ratio with a caring teacher is the best learning environment for children. The other possibility is that people who tend to home school are the type whose children would also score well if they were in conventional school, due to their God-given intelligence and stable, stimulating homes.

This is not to say that there is not a wide range in home schoolers' scores, just as there would be in the general population.

Why Did My Child Test Poorly?

There are several possibilities. Perhaps he is a slow starter and has not reached the physical and mental maturity necessary for academic success. Perhaps there are learning disabilities . . . a real possibility, although many educators tend to overuse it. Does your child have trouble learning? You can't beat it into him. "The wrath of man does not achieve the righteousness of God." But don't give up either. Be persistent. Try every approach possible. Often children who appear to have learning disabilities are those who have been or are expected to perform beyond their maturity level. Take off the pressure to perform, but don't remove discipline from his life. This child needs a consistent order to his day and loving, reasonable expectations for his behavior. Talk to other parents who have similar situations and continue to look for new approaches.

Perhaps your child scored poorly because he just doesn't test well, and you know he knows a lot more than the results showed.

Perhaps you are home teaching because your child was doing poorly in conventional school. In this case, it will take time to bring him up to grade level.

In all of these cases, a poorer-than-hoped-for test score is no reason to be discouraged, disgusted, or depressed. On the other hand, perhaps your child tested poorly because you didn't do your job. Some self-examination may be in order.

❑ *Was I diligent to be sure that I spent a proper amount of time schooling?* Is it possible that I tried to continue doing all of the things that I did before I began home teaching, and couldn't fit the schooling in? Maybe I was too busy helping others. It may be that I have three toddlers, and it just hasn't worked out. Maybe I was selfish and undisciplined and neglected my responsibility to my child.

❏ *Is it possible that the time I did spend school-ing was not used effectively?* Perhaps I catered too much to my child, allowing him to decide what would be studied and when. After all, "Foolishness is bound up in the heart of a child." Children do not naturally know what's good for them. It is the adult that needs to have the long-range view, and set and enforce educational goals to ensure that the child will be well-equipped as an adult.

❏ *Perhaps my child just didn't cooperate with what I asked him to do.* If I don't consistently require obedience from him, he can easily avoid schoolwork by dawdling and fooling around and complaining. This will be addressed in Chapter 12.

I must prayerfully consider these possibilities. If I find that I have been negligent, I must bring my own life, my own mothering into obedience to God. Perhaps it is best for me to make other arrangements for my child's schooling. Perhaps I can continue to home teach after I put my own priorities in the proper focus. In any event, my own obedience to God comes first.

Do Home-Taught Children Show Any Special Strengths or Weaknesses?

Home-taught children tend to score *highest* in reading. This is a nice trend to see, because if a per-son can read well he can then find out anything else he needs to know.

Home schoolers tend to score *lowest* in math computation. These scores are often significantly lower than those in math concepts and problem-solving. Many are unable to complete the math computation portion in the allotted time, although they often know the material and do very well on the part they do com-plete. This may be because we tend to stress accuracy and understanding over speed and sheer volume of work . . . Rightly so, I believe.

However, part of the reason may be that our children tend to waste a lot of time and are unaccustomed to putting their hand to a not-so-pleasant task and cranking out the work. In a home with a limited number of children, fooling around does not present the discipline problem it does in a class of thirty, so we tend to put up with it. I'm not for taking all the fun out of lesson time, but it is important to teach our children to be diligent as well.

I'm making an effort this year to speed my eight-year-old daughter up in math. For many of her drill assignments I set an appropriate time limit, and make *sure* that getting the work done on time is more pleasant that not getting it done on time, to see if that would bring the score up! (It did! And she was so tickled with herself when she finished that part of the test before her allotted time was up! It made all those tears worth it to both of us.)

Similarly, home schoolers generally score significantly lower on the capitalization and punctuation sections of the language battery than they do on the usage section. Once again, it is not understanding that is the problem but mechanics. Home school moms often do not sufficiently emphasize those skills that tend to be boring and require a certain amount of drill. Capitalization and punctuation skills may not seem to have much value for eternity, but expressing oneself properly on paper is a credit to the Lord Jesus, while poor writing habits reflect poorly on Him by making Christians appear to be ignorant. Happily, a little diligent work can easily propel your children ahead in these mechanical areas. "Do all things unto the glory of God!"

What Should My Attitude Towards Testing Be?

There is no reason for either parent or child to be anxious about achievement testing. The Bible is clear that worry is the opposite of faith. An anxious attitude will not accomplish anything, and besides, I should really want an objective evaluation of my child's academic progress. If I feel pressured, my child will pick up on it and may not do as well on the test because he is nervous or upset.

Many moms are uptight about their children taking tests because test-taking was a traumatic part of their own childhoods. Present the test to your children as a tool designed to show you what they already know. Explain to them that it will help you decide what they still need to learn. Let the child know that the heat is on you, not on him. To a home teacher, the real value of testing is that it makes you aware of any areas of strength or weakness, so that you can teach more effectively.

If properly handled, testing time can be a pleasant break in the normal school routine. The tests are really rather like a game or a puzzle, once the pressure is off.

What Should My Attitude Toward Test Scores Be?

Although most of us desire academic excellence in our children, it is not the primary reason we have chosen to home school. We home school because we desire to obey God, and have decided before Him to use this method to bring up our children in the nurture and admonition of the Lord.

We desire first of all that our children will come to know Christ as Savior and Lord, and that they will continue to love, obey, and trust Him. We desire that they will learn to be loving, kind, merciful and forgiving towards their family as well as towards the rest of the world. We desire that they will develop the courage and conviction to stand for God in the midst of a crooked and perverse generation. We desire that they will mature into responsible adults: husbands, wives, fathers, mothers, employers, employees, neighbors, citizens, and members of the body of Christ.

Achievement tests do not measure any of these. They do not measure godliness or character, nor do they measure creativity, communication skills, sense of humor, general knowledge, and a host of other valuable traits. Therefore, whether our children fare well or ill when tested, we need to keep the matter in the proper perspective.

Relax. Don't forget that the test measures only what it was designed to measure: academic performance in selected areas. The things that are most important in God's eyes are not and cannot be measured by an achievement test.

9

Scheduling: A Glimpse of Reality

"If you aim at nothing,
You are sure to hit it."
— Smart archer

G enerally people fall into two categories with respect to their overall approach to scheduling. We tend to be either more *structured* or *unstructured* by nature. This does not mean that the structured types always are on top of things, nor does it mean that the unstructured types are always on the bottom, but it is a description of our general approach to life.

Both approaches have their home schooling advantages and disadvantages. The *structureds* have a tendency to shoot too high, feel like they can never quite do it right, and may fall apart if life becomes too unpredictable. They may be overwhelmed by teaching several grades at once, or planning around a toddler. On the other hand, they are good at goal-setting, self-discipline, and organizing their days.

Unstructureds, bless their hearts, tend to have

very broad and noble goals but no concrete means of accomplishing them. The day is over before they had time to do anything with it. Not only did they not get much done, they don't really know what they did or did not get done since they had no real plans for the day. The advantage is that unstructured people are better able to go with the flow and adapt to changes.

We need to find a happy medium. We do need to plan our weeks and days in order to accomplish our long-range goals, but we need to be flexible since our world is unpredictable. *Structureds* need to realize that kids will get sick, the phone will ring, the baby will cry, our neighbors will need us, people will drop in, etc., but that's okay. *Unstuctureds* need to make a plan so that progress is made in between all these events.

Many books on home schooling try to help by presenting a "typical schedule." I have found that I am not typical and most of my friends aren't either. It usually takes me several weeks each year to figure out a schedule that will work. Each year is different. I have kids in different grades than last year. Perhaps I am trying a new chore system. My husband's work schedule may have changed. Maybe I had a baby, or maybe the baby is now into everything, or whatever.

It is important to remember that there is no ideal schedule for every family. The plan of attack will not only vary some from house to house, but within your home it will also vary from year to year and even day to day.

Most families find it works best to concentrate on the academics in the morning, and depending on the age of the children, to use the afternoon for free play, independent reading, projects, chores, and/or outside classes, etc. The children are usually at their best in the morning, and probably Mom is too.

Here are some ideas from some of our favorite home teaching moms. What we want to do is give you a kind of smorgasbord from which to choose a plan that may be a good starting-place for your situation.

Carolyn Neal

This is Carolyn's ninth year home teaching. She has two daughters ages seventeen and twelve, two sons ages nine and three, and a husband with a crazy schedule.

"Scheduling has been a major problem for me in the past, and a recurring annoyance in the present. While I can organize a one-time activity, working consistently for any period of time with a schedule for daily life has always evaded me.

"I have tried to order my life in such a way as to build a good relationship with my husband when he is available. Both of us have had to be flexible on this point in order to make room for home school. It seems to me that this is one of the advantages of home schooling: flexibility for the continually fluctuating family.

"The great difficulty of ultra-flexibility is ultra-nothing-done. We can graph our progress more clearly within the confines of a schedule. (I'm speaking as an unstructured person. To those for whom structure flows in their very blood, I'm sure structure holds many more rewards.)

"Therefore, I have found several aids to the progress problem while decreasing the scheduling problem. The first is commitment . . . both long-term and short-term . . . a realistic commitment to a certain amount of daily work and a certain amount of work done within a year's time. This meant that before the year began, I decided how much I wanted to cover with each child in each subject. Looking through the material, I decided what I felt was of top importance, what was nice to have, and what I'd just as soon skip. Then I tried to balance this off against the number and amount of daily assignments.

"Now, our daily schedule is from the time we wake up and finish breakfast until each person's work is done. This can vary from 11:00 A.M. to 3:00 or 4:00 P.M. I think scheduling is highly individual to each

family. If some order or goal-making is not done, everyone will tend to feel (and they may be right) that nothing was done."

Susan White

Susan has been home teaching for five years. She has two daughters, ages nine and seven

"We are in the process right now of falling into this year's schedule. It looks like this is going to be the plan:

8:30	9:00	Bible together. (I'm doing it first to convey its importance.)
9:00	9:30	Math; individual assignments.
9:30	10:00	Daughter number one works independently (typing, piano practice), while daughter number two does chores with me.
10:00	10:30	Both girls play in backyard while I have a quiet time.
10:30	11:00	Language arts; individual assignments.
11:00	11:30	Social studies, science, computer together (each week is different).
11:30	12:00	Daughter number one does chores with me, while daughter number two is free.
12:00	2:00	Lunch break. This time is unpredictable due to my husband's lunch schedule. He likes to come home for lunch if he can. It's nice

to spend the time together as a family, but the uncertainty is hard on my structured tendencies.

2:00   2:30   Read aloud with the girls.

"I tried to arrange the subjects roughly in order of how important they were to get done each day. That way if we don't get to everything, at least we did the important things. In my heart, a quiet time is a priority, but it just doesn't work out for me to do it earlier in the day. Language arts are more important, in my opinion, than they appear on the schedule, but as both of my daughters are avid readers and natural spellers, I don't feel we need to spend much time on these areas.

"We are not strict about ending each activity on the half-hour, but usually quit when we are at a natural stopping-place. This schedule is our goal for each day. I'm sure we never follow it exactly, but we come pretty close about three out of five days."

Valerie Caperino

This is Valerie's third year home teaching. She has three daughters, ages ten, eight, and five.

"Our schedule has gone through numerous revisions, but usually each one is better than the last. I am pretty satisfied with our present schedule, which has been basically the same since the beginning of this school year.

8:30   9:30   Devotions, unit study (science or social studies).

9:30   12:00   Individual work—
                Deborah (age ten): Two pages math, reading in library related

> to unit study, God's World, pro-
> jects related to unit study or Girl
> Scout badges.
> Melissa (age eight): Two pages
> each of math, phonics, spelling,
> and reading.

12:00	1:00	Lunch and chores.
1:00	?	Basically unscheduled. Girls fin-
ish schoolwork, do chores, play,
while I keep up with paperwork,
do laundry, etc.; or we run
errands or visit friends."

Jane Langley

Jane is in her second year home teaching. Her sons are ages nine, six, and four, and her daughter is ten months old.

8:30	9:00	Devotions ("big" boys sit beside
Jane on the couch, four-year-old
on her lap, baby crawls all over
everybody while we read Bible
story books together, memorize
verses, etc.).
9:00	11:30	Baby naps while boys move to
kitchen table for school. Nine-
year-old works from a list of
assignments, in any order he
chooses, asking for help when he
needs it. When he is done, Jane
goes over his work with him and
they do spelling together. Jane
works individually with the six-
year-old on phonics for half an
hour. Then he has a break. After
that they work on math and

about two days a week they work on reading. The four-year-old can basically do what he likes as long as he isn't a nuisance. Sometimes he has school with quiet activities at the table, sometimes he plays.

12:00	4:00	Informal learning activities such as reading, drawing, educational games; playing indoors and out; visiting with friends.

Susie Arevalo

Susan has five years experience in home teaching. Her daughters are ten years old, eight years old, and three months. Her sons are ages six and two.

The Arevalos are involved in the Advanced Training Institute of America, a home school program available through Institute in Basic Youth Conflicts. The following schedule has worked the best for them, but they are constantly flexing with the new baby and the little boys.

	5:00	Mom and Dad get up.
6:00	6:30	Kids get up and dress.
6:30	7:00	Bible reading.
7:00	7:30	Breakfast.
7:30	8:00	One child washes dishes while others pick up their rooms. Mom starts laundry and straightens up, but no cleaning at this time. Dad plays piano.
8:00	9:00	Dad goes to work, girls do memo-

		ry work, while Mom does memory work with six-year-old or reads to both little boys.
9:00	11:00	Wisdom booklet (unit studies), research, boys play in room or outside.
11:00	12:00	Math, grammar or spelling, and handwriting.
12:00	1:00	Lunch (afterwards, one girl washes dishes, the others play).
1:00	2:00	Quiet time for Mom, girls read or occasionally catch up on studies, Mom reads to little boys, then two-year-old naps. Sometimes Mom reads to all.
2:00	3:00	Kids can play now. Two days a week the girls have grammar or spelling at this time.
3:00	4:30	Crafts, baking or sewing at least once a week.
4:30	5:30	Straighten up before Dad comes home.

Patti Feliciano

Patti is a fifth-year home schooler. She has three girls aged ten, eight, and two. Patti's husband is home in the mornings, and she finds she can get more schoolwork done in the afternoon while he is at work and the little one is napping.

Cindy Bates

Cindy is in her fourth year home teaching two daughters ages nine and six.

Cindy has school every morning except Monday. On Monday she cleans house in the morning and has school in the afternoon. She is happy with this schedule because it gives her time to get the house together after the weekend, and if something comes up on that afternoon, she has only missed one day of school, and can usually make up the work during the rest of the week.

Ginger Frank

This is Ginger's second year home teaching her six-year-old son.

9:00	9:30	Mom reads aloud.
9:30	10:15	Phonics program.
10:15	10:45	Snack and recess.
10:45	11:15	Bible or character development.
11:15	11:45	Educational games, science experiments, and other hands-on activities.
11:45	12:00	Craft or stories.

The father does math with his son on Tuesday evenings and Saturday mornings for about an hour. Math-related topics are also discussed informally during the course of the day.

Vicky Peters

Vicky has been home schooling for three years, and has three sons aged eleven, eight, and four, and a daughter aged two.

6:30	7:00	Chores with Dad.
7:00	7:30	Breakfast, informal math with Dad.
8:00	8:30	Prayer and Bible study with Mom.
8:30	9:00	Break.
9:00	10:30	The eleven-year-old watches the little ones while Mom does reading and math with the eight-year-old, or the eight-year-old may watch them while Mom works with the older one. The older child does most of his work independently, while the younger does most with Mom. Mom tries to spend some time with each of the little ones during the morning so that they don't feel left out. She plays with the baby or reads to the four-year-old while the big boys do some work independently.
10:30	11:00	Break.
11:00	12:00	Read aloud— usually something to do with social studies.
12:00	12:30	Lunch.
12:30	4:00	Journal writing, art (directed or non-directed), music and play.

Cheryl and Gregory Falconer

Cheryl and Gregory have been home teaching their daughter, age ten, for two years. Their situation is different in that the father is disabled and at home, and the mother works two school days a week. They have tried to divide the subject areas so that each teaches what they are most comfortable with.

8:00   9:00   Piano practice.

9:00   10:00   Aerobics with TV show.

10:00   1:30   Academics and half-hour lunch break.
Monday, Wednesday, and Friday: math and social studies with Mom, and English with Dad. This division of labor is not followed strictly; sometimes one or the other parent does more or less. Tuesday and Thursday: reading, English and science with Dad.

1:30   3:00   Free time. Cheryl usually reads.

3:00   4:30   A friend visits on Tuesday and Thursday; then they both go to classes at the city parks and recreation program. They swim in home pool on other days.

It is important that you do what you can to make it possible to follow a schedule. This means informing all of your friends and relations (sweetly, of course) that since you now have a job, you won't be able to receive visitors or calls during school hours. For those calls that you cannot prevent or postpone, we have found an answer phone to be a real blessing. Try to let people know that you have this wonderful little device in order to help *them*. This way they will not have to worry about disturbing your class time, nor will they be frustrated by a busy signal. If you use a machine, please be courteous enough to return calls at the soonest possible time. It is rude to say you will return a call and then not do it. It is also a lie.

Schedule the rest of your life, as much as possible, around your school schedule, rather than the other way around. Try to make doctors' appointments after school, as well as other events within your control. Sometimes you will want to interrupt school for other activities, but it's better to make that the exception rather than the rule. Remember, you want a balance between flexibility and rigidity.

Flexibility within your school schedule is very important. One of the beauties of home teaching is that we can take advantage of the spontaneity of the moment. Spend the day doing science if everyone is excited about it. Keep reading an exciting book if no one can stand to stop without finding out what happens. If you are studying pronouns and a strange blue polka-dot bug crawls across the table, by all means drop English and check out the bug! When it comes to school, variety is the spice of life; but on the other hand, a diet of spices alone is neither tasty nor nutritious. So once again, keep a balance.

10

Teaching Several Grades at Once

Two's company, three's a crowd;
Four's outrageous and five's too
loud.
— The Voice of Experience

H ere is the chapter you've all been waiting for! Before you get your hopes up, please keep in mind that in any area where individual human beings are involved there are no pat answers. I have taught differently every year, depending on the ages of my kids. I will give you some ideas on how to look at the problem and some possible solutions, and then you will need to pray and think and experiment to find out what works best for you.

To begin, it is important to remember what it is you are trying to accomplish. I know that sounds silly, but it is amazing how we can get so bogged down in the lesson plans, books and techniques that we lose sight of the goal. For most of us the goal is to instill godly values in our children, and to teach them the skills they will need to become productive adults. In light of this, here are some things to remember:

❏ Academically, the "Three Rs" are the most important things for the kids to learn. In order to function well as adults, they must know how to read well, express themselves well in writing, using good spelling and proper grammar, and be able to solve any kind of practical mathematical problem they may come up against. This is the same foundation given to our forefathers which served them so well.

❏ Although each state and each curriculum designer has a scope and sequence (a plan that tells what is covered in each subject at each level) which includes science and social studies, these things can be learned in any order and pretty much at any time. At some point each child should learn about the history of our country, and what molecules are, but not at the expense of reading, writing and math.

A lady came to me with a daughter who was fifteen years old, couldn't read beyond a fourth grade level, couldn't multiply or divide, and was a freshman in a local public high school. How she had gotten that far is another story, but here she was, and her mother needed a curriculum. I talked to the girl and found that she really did want to catch up, and was willing to go back as far as necessary to do so.

I began to lay out a remedial plan for them to follow. The plan included phonics, reading aloud, and basic math, to be followed with grammar and spelling. Then the mom asked me what we would use for an American history text and for biology, since that is what she was supposed to have that year . . . In order to graduate she needed x number of units. I felt very frustrated. I explained to the mother that if she wanted to cover American history, she could get a fourth grade level book for her daughter to read, or use other books on the subject for part of her program of reading aloud to her, but there was absolutely no point in talking about high school science if the girl could hardly read! Remember: First things first!

❑ In our American public school system there are very few *real* academic standards. You must meet certain criteria to enter the four-year college of your choice, but even these vary depending on the college and the reason you are going there; i.e., athletes often need not be as astute as others, etc. On few levels do students have to master certain subjects or skills in order to move on to the next.

Junior colleges will take just about anyone, regardless of whether they have completed high school. Junior colleges are set up to teach basic math to those who need it as well as elementary English. Therefore, kids are passed on to the next grade regardless of their ability to do the work on that level. Kids that can't do the work are put in the slow track, and everyone hopes that maybe this time they will pick up what they have missed thus far. What happens emotionally to these kids who have become losers in the system is another story. It may be that some of you reading this book were losers in the system and that is why you have chosen to home teach your own children.

"Graduating from High School with a B average" no longer means as much as it used to mean. For this reason colleges primarily depend on objective standardized testing for their entrance qualifications.

All this to say that in the public and private sector, there *is* no standard scope and sequence for subjective areas such as history and science. At some point children should study American history and understand our government. They should also have a clear picture of the history of the world. It is very important for them to see that the external events of history are the symptoms of spiritual and moral battles in the hearts of people living as nations.

You can teach these subjects any way you want to and not worry about being caught up, just so the kids are taught what they need to know. Each state, school and teacher presents these things in a different order.

In the foundational areas of reading, writing, and math, we need to make sure that our kids are *proficient*. We must give them a base on which anything else can be built. If we do this, we will be doing a better job than the schools are doing, even if it takes us a little longer.

With these things in mind, you can then have more flexibility as you plan your curriculum for several levels at once. For example, if you have a second, fourth, and fifth-grader, you can read a fourth or fifth grade level social studies text aloud to them all and do the questions orally. You can have the two older kids in the same level science program (a choice based on their reading level). Let the second-grader watch when lab activities are done, but otherwise you need no formal science curriculum for him, since he will be spending more time on foundational subjects. All the children can study Bible together.

If you have a sixth- and an eighth-grader, there is no reason to not have them both in seventh grade life science, if the sixth-grader is a good reader (another plug for a good foundation). The next year they can both do earth science. Double up wherever you can on the subjective areas.

Confessions of a Home Schooling Mom

Here is my situation and what I am doing this year.

My oldest, David, age sixteen, is in tenth grade this year. Last year for ninth grade I had him on a correspondence school program, and he made about one and a half year's progress in one year. This year he is doing algebra and biology at home three days a week, has taken driver's education and driver's training through our school, and is taking three classes at the local junior college. For the college classes he is receiving both college and high school credit. He is a good student and needs little teaching from me. I grade his science and tell him to get busy, and look over his college work before he hands it in. He corrects his algebra and does pretty well with some occasional nagging from me. David is a voracious reader, spending about ten hours a week at it.

Nathan, my number two son, is almost fourteen and is in eighth grade. In times past we have had trouble getting him to be diligent about doing his work, but we have seen improvement this year. He does math, English and science about three days a week and history, literature and Bible about twice a week. I make sure he keeps working and correct his work, giving direction as needed. If he needs help in math, my husband helps him in the evening, since this is my weak area. He usually works every morning from 9:00 to 12:00. He reads on his own about two or three hours a week.

Daniel will be twelve soon and is in the sixth grade. He is the main reason I decided to home teach. After two years in school I saw that he needed a year off, so I took him out, let him play and explore his own interests for a year, then began again the following year. He is doing well in sixth grade work, which is where he should be for his age. He has the same school schedule as the girls. We begin at 8:30 A.M. in the living room for our story time. I usually read aloud from two books. One has to do with history (Bob Jones University Press Heritage Studies text, Landmark books, the Little House books, etc.) and the other exposes the kids to different types of literature (missionary biography, the Narnia series, *Swiss Family Robinson*, *Cricket in Times Square*, *The Phantom Tollboth*, *Treasure Island*, etc.). We adjourn after an hour of reading and go upstairs to start our other work. Daniel does one lesson in his math book each day, one page of handwriting, and two pages in his spelling/language book. Sometimes he works in a map skills book. He is very pokey about getting his work done. He loves science, so I give him science books to read on his own and to do when his other work is done, because we are fortunate to get the other done in that amount of time. At 11:30 the kids like to watch "Square One," a special math program on public television. I let them watch it if we have gotten our other work done. Daniel likes to read in bed at night and probably reads about three or four hours a week.

Joy, my oldest daughter is nine years old. She has always been bright, curious, and active. When she was five, she showed no interest in words, numbers or letters, so I decided to wait until she was six to start school with her. When she was six, we began kindergarten material and went very slowly. She still didn't seem to care about learning to read. We were halfway through kindergarten when she was seven. She was very artistic, had lots of questions, and still wrote her name backwards.

In the meantime, her little sister Ariana who was five was raring to go. "What is that word, Mommy?" "I know what that letter is, it's an E!" "I have three A's in my name." My sister, who lives five blocks away, had decided to home teach her daughter, who is the same age as Ariana. I asked her if she would teach Ariana too, and I would pay her. So while Joy and I plugged along finishing kindergarten and going slowly on into first grade, Ariana forged ahead. To make a long story short, I began them both in second grade this year.

Both girls have done very well. Joy is faster at getting her work done, but is not as good at following written directions (she is an auditory learner). In all outside activities (Sunday school, Girl Scouts, etc.), she is a fourth-grader. Together we do math, handwriting, spelling and language, or reading every day. They have been clamoring for science, so I have gotten some little workbooks for them to do if their other work is done.

This year Joy has made great strides in her reading. I just finished testing her and her grade equivalent score was 6.1. She was thrilled and so was I! I moved her up to a fourth grade reader, which is a challenge for her, but makes her feel like a million bucks. If I work with her, I think she will handle it very well.

Ariana is almost eight and is in second grade. She recently began a third grade reader. She is an eager learner and likes to do extra pages in math.

Both girls can listen for hours to stories, and are just beginning to read for their own pleasure.

Peter is six years old. He also has not shown any real interest in words, numbers or letters until recently. He is quiet and cuddly and full of ideas and inventions. He loves to be read to and has a long attention span for listening to stories and poems. He is just now attempting to draw, can put Legos together, and can write his name.

Luke is almost five years old. He is as busy as a bee, loves to be read to, but not longer than about a half an hour. He draws stick figures and letters on the sidewalk with chalk and tells me what it says. He knows that both of our names begin with "Lu," and he recognizes Peter's name. He can count things in Spanish and English.

While I'm doing school with the older kids, the little boys are in and out of the school room, playing outside, or watching the educational TV channel.

I think that I will begin both little boys in kindergarten next year. It is easier for me to teach that way, and I have reason to believe that they will both be ready at that time. I will play it by ear when the time comes. That is what home schooling is all about, right?

Give yourself the freedom to consider your children's academic levels before their ages. It may be that you can do some "bunching" in foundational areas as well.

I do not spend lots of time in preparation. (Maybe this book should have been called *Confessions of a Home Schooling Mom.*) To be quite honest, I sort of fly by the seat of my pants. I know that we are supposed to stay up every night till 11 planning the next day's lessons, or all day Saturday planning the week's lessons, but this is not what I do.

When it is time for the academic part of our day, we sit down and I ask the kids to do their handwriting first. While they are doing that, I get out my teacher's manual for English. I go over the lesson for today, and when the kids are done with their handwriting, we do English. While they are working on their English assignment, I am looking at spelling or reading. While they are doing that, I look at the math lesson, and so on. If it turns out that there was more to that lesson than I was counting on, I skip that subject for today and plan extra time for it tomorrow.

Sometimes we will spend a lot of time each day on spelling and math, for example, and little or no time on English and reading. Then for a while we will spend the bulk of our time on those subjects and back off on the others.

I ad lib in other ways too. My Bob Jones University Press reading lessons include three parts: the actual reading, a phonics or grammar lesson, and workbook reinforcement. On the first day we do three days' lessons of the reading part, then the next day do three days phonics and grammar, and on the third day do all the workbook pages. There is more than one way to skin a cat, so be creative!

If one child needs extra help, get the other kids going on their work and give the needy one some time. On a day where you can't stand over them every minute (like if you don't get the laundry taken care of, the whole family may be arrested for indecent exposure) or you need to run errands, write out what pages you expect them to get done and check it over during lunch.

Make good use of non-school time. Talk to your kids. One day we saw a sign announcing the centennial for our town. After we talked about that, we got into a long lesson on Latin. We talked about all *uni, duo, tri, qua, quint, sept, oct, nov,* and *dec* words. Identify the trees on your street and study them. Study your pets and their parasites. One of the very best things you can give your kids is an active curiosity. Take the time to pull over to the side of the road to find out what crop is growing there. Pull down some of those bumpy leaves to see why they are like that. If you don't know, try to find out. Some of your best teaching will be spontaneous, so keep your ears and eyes open.

Remember, too, that you don't have to do *all* of the wonderful things you hear about in workshops and seminars. Do what you *can*. God knows, and you ought to know, that all you can do is your best. Do what you can do to the best of your ability, and don't dwell on what you are not able to do right now. There is absolutely no point in it. Guilt uses up precious energy and, if you are like me, you can't afford to waste any. You are probably doing a great job, and I think you are wonderful!

But What About Babies and Toddlers?

Well, it is definitely true that little kids make home schooling more interesting. I remember a time a while back when Peter was three and Luke was about twenty months. They had been in and out of the "school room" all morning. Lukey had been getting into things, pulling books off the shelf, and wanting to draw on the kids' papers, and Peter was whining and wanting to get in and out of my lap. They finally went out and after a while it was quiet. I rejoiced in the tranquility, forgetting that if you have toddlers, silence is not golden. I came out to find that Peter had flushed a truck down the toilet and Luke had eaten all my make-up! He had bitten off and chewed up two lipsticks, dumped and tasted my foundation, and put teeth marks in my blush! It didn't seem to affect him, except that the next day's diapers were rather colorful, but it really affected me! I was so upset, plus we had to take up and reseat the toilet in order to remove the truck!

Not very much has been written about how to handle little ones when you are trying to home school. I think this is because men write most of the books, and because there aren't any sure-fire solutions. Let's face it . . . although toddlers are adorable, they are not easy. Whole books have been written on the subject of how to live with them, train them, feed them, and survive them. Add all that to home schooling two or more big kids and we are up to our ears in trouble! I speak from experience.

The more kids you have, the harder it is to keep track of where the little ones are. My two youngest have gotten into more trouble than all the others combined. I think this is because we are in a bigger house with more kids, and I am home schooling and I can't see where they are. I praise the Lord that none of them have eaten poisonous substances, but Peter *almost* fell out a second story window, and *did* fall six feet off the back porch. They've dumped flour, oil, baking soda, honey, and eggs on the kitchen floor at different times, and walked with painted feet across the living room carpet. Each of the little boys has been brought back to me by a neighbor who has found them at the busy intersection at the end of our block . . . They had decided to visit someone and I hadn't missed them. I really do believe in guardian angels! How often I have felt that I was tapped on the shoulder and reminded to check the little one, only to find him on the brink of disaster. I think most mothers have experiences like these, home schooling or not. I write all this to let you know that you are not alone. It is God who protects our babies, and it is a miracle that any of them survive.

"Then are you saying that we should forget home teaching if we have toddlers?" Oh, no . . . I just want to encourage you to be realistic. If we start by being realistic about the problem, then we can work on some possible solutions. Remember, this is a *survivor's* guide. I've made it this far, and I consider myself to be the acid test. We may never get written up in *Redbook* as Wondermom of the Year, but hopefully we will make it through one day, and then another, and then another, and so on until we are old ladies. Then our kids will come back to us and say, "Mom, I don't know how you *ever* did it!" and we can look very wise and say, "Hmm . . . I did it one day at a time, that's how."

Now we will get down to some ideas. First for babies, then for the bigger ones.

❑ It is a good idea to get your baby into some sort of routine during the day. Most babies take a morning and an afternoon nap. Try to teach your older kids during this time rather than doing the housework. Teaching needs quiet, but the dishes don't.

❑ If the baby is not a napper, make good use of your swing, playpen, backpack, front carrier and floor blanket. It is my feeling, however, that if he is fussing all that time he probably needs a nap and should be put to bed. It is very difficult to teach if your baby uses your breast as a nose warmer all morning.

❑ Teach each of the older kids in fifteen-minute turns, while the other is walking the baby in the stroller around the house or up and down the sidewalk.

❑ While you work one-on-one with one child, pay the other sibling to baby-sit (25¢ per hour) the toddler. Roles can be switched to work with the other sibling. This could be good learning time for future baby-sitting jobs (and motherhood and fatherhood).

❑ When they begin to crawl and walk, give them things to get into so they don't get into *your* things. Fill a basket and a box with toys for them to dump out and scatter around. Put plastic containers and dishes in a bottom cupboard and drawer for them to unload. They

will think they are getting into all sorts of mis-
chief, but you will know better.

❑ When they get to be very steady on their feet,
the kitchen sink becomes a real help. Put a
chair (or chairs depending on the number of
kids) with the back to the counter in front of
the sink. Put warm water and bubbles into the
sink, give the toddler a ton of Tupperware, and
ask him to please wash the dishes. This is usually good for at least forty-five minutes of peace.
The floor and the child will both get wet, but
since neither will melt, it's a small price to pay.
Besides, the floor probably needed mopping
anyway. Be sure that you put the soap bottle
out of reach, as well as any glass items.

❑ Play dough is a messy option. My husband
can't stand the stuff. No matter how I handle
it, it gets in the carpet. You might try it on the
patio, and then have them remove their shoes
before coming in.

❑ Television. I know . . . that's terrible! Here you
are, being so noble, home schooling your
school-aged kids, while the toddlers are sitting
like little zombies in the den watching "He-
Man." That is not really what I meant. I was
raised without a TV, and up until five months
ago we never had one. We now have a little
black and white. We only allow it to be tuned
to the public television station. Most of the
time it is so boring no one even wants to
watch it, but the little boys enjoy some of the
programs in the morning. I feel that since it is
a small fraction of their life and experience, it
is not harmful, and it is a big help to me during school time.

❑ For preschoolers who clamor to "have school
too," it is a good idea to sit down and read to

them for ten minutes or so before you begin schoolwork with the big ones. Plan for the older children to do their chores or have independent reading during this time. This makes the little ones feel that they are not being left out of all the attention. You can also get some "color the triangle red" type workbooks to do with them a little each day. I do not recommend a formal pre-kindergarten program. You need more lessons to plan like you need measles!

❏ Hire someone to come in for two hours a day or two or three hours three mornings a week to run herd on the little ones. Pay as you would a baby-sitter. Have this person take the littlest ones for a walk, give them a bath, supervise their play, or do a craft. This person could watch and change the baby and bring him to you to be nursed if needed. This frees you to really be with the kids you are teaching for a consistent block of time.

❏ If you have a close friend who also has toddlers and a school-age child the same age as yours, you might consider a swap. Maybe she would rather have the little ones for the morning and you would rather teach, or vice versa. Such arrangements can work well if there is agreement in areas such as discipline, nutrition and expectations of each other.

Remember to be flexible. You *will not* be able to have a schedule that is the same every day. Have long-range goals that you keep in mind over daily goals. Every day will be different, so you must expect it, accept it and even plan for it. If you can decide ahead of time that this is not a problem, then you will be ahead of the game. Don't waste energy trying to change the unchangeable. Look at your situation, be realistic about it, and then work with it.

Every week is different. There are doctor's appointments, sickness, out-of-town visitors, and holidays. There are good days, bad days, and crazy days. Every year it is different. One year it's toddlers and potty training, and in no time it's teenagers and all that goes with them. This year maybe you have money, but maybe next year you won't. Now you may have three kids, but you may be blessed with six. Nothing stays the same except the faithfulness of God. Put your energies into the things that will matter twenty years from now and for eternity. Don't get excited or upset about things that won't matter tomorrow, or next week, or a month from now or even next year. Keep an eternal perspective by looking to the Lord. Read His Word to find out what the truly important things are from *His* point of view, and concentrate on *them.*

11

Help! It's Not Working!

"Uh . . . We think he is one of those late bloomers."
— Worried mother

T he idea of home schooling is wonderful. Most children really excel and become feathers in their mother's caps. Books on the subject are full of examples of kids with problems who came through with flying colors. You don't read about the home schooled child who scores low, refuses to write, can't read at age eleven, and who simply can't understand fractions.

They do exist. Their mothers are trying to remain calm. Every day they wonder if perhaps this wouldn't have happened if the child had been in school, and then console themselves by saying it probably would have been worse if they had. But who knows?

How do you hide the awful truth from your mother-in-law who was against home schooling in the first place? How long will your husband be patient and understanding? He believes that you are doing your best, but is your best good enough?

What if this child had to enter school right now? You *know* it would be a disaster. No way would he be caught up in three months. Everyone will think your child is either dense, or the victim of a fanatical and misguided mother. We try very hard not to think these thoughts, but if we are to fight and win, we must admit there is a problem to fight.

Thousands of kids in the school systems of our country have the same problems and much worse. If, say, 15 percent of all kids have some learning difficulties, it is inevitable that some of these children will be home taught. As a caring mother, you are much more likely to be able to make headway with a child who learns differently. Such a child in the system is often labeled as a loser, but you can work with the problems while supporting and encouraging the character and uniqueness of your child. All of the tools available to teachers in the school system are also available to you, and you can give your child far more time, love, discipline, and support than can be given in a classroom. Take heart!

Reading

If there is one thing every child *must* learn, it is how to read. After all, illiteracy is the primary cause of poverty, crime, delinquency, and disease, right? Well, no. Sin is the cause of most of that, but reading *is* important.

What do we know about reading? Well, we all know that *Johnny can't read* because he wasn't taught phonics. We shudder to think of the fate of the kids in the local school who are being taught *sight reading*. Such is the decline of our nation's educational system! So, the first thing on the list of curriculum to buy is a good phonics program. The ones most popular among home schoolers seem to be: *Sing, Spell, Read, and Write, Play 'N Talk* (my favorite), *Professor Phonics*, and *The Writing Road to Reading*. We are going to do it *right!* We've waited until the child is seven, and now we are ready to really go after it.

But I have at least five friends with ten- and eleven-year-old children who are not reading. Most of these are girls. They can barely remember the sounds of the letters, and by the time they have "sounded out" a word, they can't remember what the word is. Four of these kids have been taught phonics using *Sing, Spell, Read and Write* for at least two years. The kids are frustrated, the mothers are frantic, and the younger siblings are passing them up using the same program.

All of these children are very bright. They remember every detail of a story that is read to them. They can memorize long poems and passages of Scripture. Many are very artistic and can draw very well.

Kids like this meet the description of a *strong right hemisphere learner*. What does that mean? Don't worry. It doesn't mean there is anything wrong with your child. It just means he learns differently than the majority of the population. Right-brained children tend to be creative rather than logical. They have difficulty making associations and transferring learned information from one experience to the next. For example with phonics, such a child can make the sounds but not read the words. Even if the child can figure out the words, he needs to sound them out each time he comes to them and loses the sense of the passage. In math, he may know his addition facts but not know how to apply addition in problem-solving.

Here are some things to try if you have a child like this. Remember, most kids learn better with phonics, but this kind of child needs a different approach. No philosophy or method of man, no matter how wonderful, is perfect. Only the Word of God applies to every person in every situation.

❑ Use a sight reading method to teach reading. Remember your goal: not to teach your child phonics, but to teach him to read. Phonics is merely one method of teaching reading. If phonics isn't doing the trick, don't feel obliged to stick with it. (*Play 'N Talk* is a phonics program with a lot of visual materials and is therefore better than most programs for both types of learners.)

The *look-say* method was developed to teach deaf children to read, and it was a real breakthrough. However, some educators with their heads in the clouds decided, "Wow! This is working so well for deaf people, just think how great it would be for normal people." Wrong. That's like saying that since crutches help people with broken legs to get around, everyone ought to use them. Deaf people can't use the phonics method because they can't hear words or sounds. They have no choice but to be visual learners rather than auditory learners. Most people employ both their ears and their eyes to transfer information to their brains. Each person generally favors one over the other. A child that is extremely visually inclined *may* do better with the look-say method, just as deaf children do.

A child who strongly favors the right hemisphere of his brain may also do better with a *sight reading* method. This will relieve him of the tedium of sounding out words and move him directly into reading.

You probably don't need to buy an entirely new curriculum, unless your entire program includes nothing but sounding out words. Use the books you already have and make flash cards of the words. Encourage the child to see the words as units. Don't ask him to sound out the words. When he asks what a word is, tell him. Use sentences from the text and print them on a piece of paper. Then have the child create the same sentences using flash cards. He can copy them on paper to emphasize proper spelling. If needed, put pictures on the word cards at first. Advance from looking at a sentence and recreating it with flash cards to hearing a sentence and recreating it with flash cards.

There is no need to stick to the traditional *baby words* used in beginning readers. It is just as easy, if not easier, to recognize a word like "gigantic" by sight as a word like "big." And besides, it will make your child who has been struggling so long and showing little progress feel like he is really getting somewhere. Build the child's sight vocabulary by labeling items around the house and pointing out roadside words.

Let the child make up a story and dictate it to you. You write it out and have the child read it aloud for several days. Use these sentences for word card matching. Then have him copy his story.

If you are using the Bob Jones University Press *Beginnings Program*, emphasize the sight-word portion of the program more heavily than the phonics. Use the word cards and all the activities that call for them. Point out the phonics principles, but don't insist that the child see words as groups of sounds.

Use singing and rhythm to teach. Find songs and clapping games for the rules of spelling and grammar. I hate to sound like a broken record, but Bob Jones University Press curriculum provides many of these.

❑ *After* the child has learned plenty of words by sight, begin pointing out how sounds within different words are the same and use the same letters. Use word families to show this: cat, fat, rat, pat, sat, tag, sag, bag, lag, etc.. Both Bob Jones University Press and *Play 'N Talk* use a word family approach.

❑ As the child begins to read, have him read into a tape recorder. After several weeks, replay the whole tape so he can hear for himself how much he has improved. This is even better than telling him he is doing well.

Remember that the brain is always growing. Once a child begins to see that words represent objects and ideas and can *read*, then he can learn phonetic principles that will help him with his spelling and with words he has never seen before.

The look-say method is what is used in those ridiculous "teach your baby to read" plans. These children really are able to learn a lot of words this way. It is the only method that will work for a very young child, because they don't have the reasoning ability to puzzle out a new word. As your child matures and sees some success with reading, he will probably gain the ability to understand and use phonics. Remember, to the experienced reader nearly all words eventually become sight words no matter how they were learned initially. It is a great handicap to depend on phonics alone for every word you encounter.

Spelling

Some people can't spell. Have you noticed? Most likely if one of your kids is a terrible speller, you won't have to look far to find a member of the family with the same problem. It is my personal opinion that poor spelling is a congenital problem and that people with this disability should be catered to. You may have guessed that I am a poor speller. So is my mom, and so are Daniel and Joy.

This doesn't mean that we don't teach spelling. It means that we need to be patient and teach them to use a dictionary also. Good spellers seem to absorb it as they read; they "just know" how to spell.

A good spelling program will teach generalizations about the way words are put together. Word families help a child remember. Bob Jones University Press and *Play 'N Talk* both use this approach, and both programs break up words into syllables, which is also a big help to poor spellers.

Poor spellers need tricks and rules to remember how to spell. Here are a few of our favorites:

- ❑ There and their and they're all begin with *the*.

- ❑ The difference between *desert* and *dessert* is that I want two helpings of *dessert*.

- ❑ Together is *to get her*.

- ❑ When two vowels go walking, the first one does the talking (usually).

- ❑ I before E except after C or when sounding like A as in *neighbor* and *weigh* (works most of the time).

- ❑ I remember how to spell schedule as "ske-dooly."

- ❑ Remember that you *hear* with your *ear* and *ear* is in *hear*.

- ❑ *Here* is in *there* and *where*, and they all are places.

Don't hesitate to resort to trickery, rhymes, and silliness to teach spelling. We poor spellers need all the help we can get. Teach your child to be an over-comer by telling him it is a weak point and by teaching him to use the dictionary. Use a good spelling pro-gram, but don't expect him to remember all those words. Don't grade for spelling on compositions, but use the words he misspells for spelling words. The Bob Jones University Press spelling program includes a journal section to help you find the words misspelled in everyday use and incorporates these words into the weekly spelling lists. If you have a computer, let your child use a word processor with a spelling checker for letter writing and final drafts.

Handwriting

Bad handwriting does not guarantee that your child will be a doctor . . . sorry. Don't let your children practice bad handwriting. If they are too young to write neatly, don't have them write. A child can go a long way in both reading and math without much writing. We've waited to start handwriting until our kids were six or seven; with Daniel I waited until nine. Susan used magnetic letters and numbers through first grade. Good handwriting comes with physical maturity. If you wait, they will do better with less struggle.

But when the time comes, *do* teach handwriting! Crummy handwriting is an embarrassment all your life. Neatness and order are virtues that should be taught on all levels and are especially obvious in handwriting. Many home schoolers are using the Bob Jones University Press precursive printing or the Scott, Foresman *D'Nealian* methods of handwriting with good success. With these programs, there seems to be an easy transition to cursive writing and less problems with reversals. It is better not to change programs in midstream, so decide which approach you want to use before you begin.

A very good program to use for children that have already been taught the standard handwriting method is *A Reason for Writing*. The children learn Scripture verses and write them on border pages each week which they decorate.

An older child with poor handwriting could be encouraged to print neatly, type, or learn calligraphy rather than settle for sloppy work.

Math

The first line of offense when it comes to fixing math difficulties is currently *manipulatives!* Manipulatives are not bribes with which you manipulate your children into doing math problems. They are objects which the child can manipulate to help him understand (visualize) the concepts of mathematics and solve problems. They are especially valuable for the kinesthetic learner (someone who learns best by *doing* rather than by seeing or hearing).

Manipulatives have their place, but they are definitely not a cure-all. In fact, some manipulatives are so sophisticated and complicated that they confuse rather than help. Your goal is not to teach your child to use manipulatives, but to teach him to use mathematics. They are tools to help learn math, just as phonics is a tool to learn reading.

Manipulatives are good for introducing a new topic and for explaining a trouble area in a different way. For example, I use blocks to teach addition, subtraction, multiplication, and division. You can probably figure out how to add and subtract with blocks. To multiply 3 x 4, have the child make three piles, each having four blocks, and then count how many blocks that took all together. Or, have him lay the blocks in a rectangle three blocks wide and four blocks long . . . This makes the transition to finding areas easy. Try to express the concept using proper math words that also make sense in English. We have four blocks, three *times*. To divide, for example 12 divided by 3, set out twelve blocks and divide them into four piles. If you are so inclined, and I am, you can teach these concepts to young children using manipulatives and small numbers, and multiplication and division won't seem so hard later.

Blocks are my favorite manipulative because they are a convenient size (large enough for childish hands to move around easily, but not so big as to become a building project), a good shape (they make rectangles, stacks, and rows), and they don't roll off the table like marbles. Coins can be used for place value and decimals. Fraction circles (paper plates) can really make fractions come alive. So often children have no trouble with math once they can see it. The teacher's manuals for Bob Jones University Press math and Modern Curriculum Press math include many great ideas for using manipulatives as you present each concept.

Most children seem to learn math most easily with wisely chosen manipulatives. These help them to understand what is actually going on behind those symbols and numbers. However, if manipulatives are confusing your child, drop them. Some kids do better with just memorizing a method and cranking out the answers. So use what works.

You must teach your child the multiplication tables! I know of no way to accomplish this without rote memorization. Don't hesitate to use flash cards. They are much less offensive to most children than page upon page of problems. Addition and subtraction can conceivably be counted on fingers and toes, but it is almost impossible to manage without knowing multiplication facts by heart. Almost all other math operations depend on these facts. If a child does not know them, he can advance beyond multiplication, but every step will be a struggle and an embarrassment. There are some helpful little tricks of the trade:

❑   7 x 8 = 56. Think of 5,6,7,8.

❑   8 x 8 fell on the floor, pick it up, it's 64.

❑   For all of the 9s the digits of the answer add up to nine and the first digit of the answer is one less than the other number with which you are multiplying. For example, 6 x 9 = 54, 5 + 4 = 9 and 5 is one less than 6.

One of the most common troubles in mathematics is that the child becomes proficient with one skill, then learns a new one and forgets the old. The only way I know to prevent this is with frequent, even daily, review. This need not be drill. One problem of each type ought to do it. If the child misses one type of problem, have him do it again, explaining each step to you. He will probably find his mistake. If he doesn't, do it with him, and then do some more until he begins to get them right.

Most math books handle one topic at a time, and so cooking up these review problems is a pain. One possibility is to get a workbook full of drill and assign as a matter of course one problem from each section per day. Some math texts (like Bob Jones University Press texts) have review problems at the back of the book that can be used the same way. Better yet, if your child is in the fourth grade or above, use the incremental math texts by Stephen D. Hake, listed in Chapter Seven on the page about recommended curriculum. All the review you need is built in.

If your high school student is unable to do basic math, get him a calculator and teach him to use it. He obviously is not headed for a career in computer programming and does not really need higher math. He can even survive very well without knowing how to add, subtract, multiply, and divide fractions, which can't be done on a calculator. He should be able to measure with fractions, however. Teach him to balance a checkbook, comparison shop, and other survival skills often taught in consumer math books. (Bob Jones University Press has a good one which includes subjects such as tithing and stewardship.)

Any More Ideas?

If you have really hit a brick wall in some area, you might also consider hiring a tutor. A fresh approach or a fresh teacher may do the trick. Look for someone who likes kids and likes to teach, rather than someone who just likes the subject matter. If possible, arrange to observe at a tutoring session prior to making a decision. You will get more mileage out of the money and time spent on a tutor if you ask for ideas and projects to work on at home. The best source of a tutor is probably word of mouth. Ask around, and if you don't hear of anything promising call a local Christian school or look in the phone book for a tutorial service.

If All Else Fails . . .

It may be that your child really does have some sort of special learning problem. If you have tried what you consider to be all the angles, it would probably be a good idea to have some special testing done. There are tests which diagnose learning problems and then provide new approaches to teaching, custom-fitted to your child. Call a local Christian school or counselor for information on what is available. Some types of testing may be available at little or no cost through your local college or university.

It may be that you should consider looking for a school program better suited to your child's needs than what you are able to offer. The Lord could have the perfect answer waiting for you in a conventional school setting or some other option. See the section "When *Not* to Home School" at the end of Chapter Ten. Don't hesitate to rattle some doorknobs to see if the Lord will open any doors. Take each child, each year, and each situation one at a time. Each is unique. Pray about it. Go to the Word. Talk to your husband. Together, look at all the information you have and make a decision. No decision of this kind is cast in cement; you can always change at the semester if you feel you have made a big mistake.

12

Making Them Do It

*Foolishness is bound up
in the heart of a child;
but the rod of correction
will drive it far from him.*
— Proverbs 22:15

I t is possible to survive unruly children until they are old enough to go to kindergarten. If, however, your kids won't mind you and you decide to home school, you had better figure out who's boss or you won't survive.

One of the questions that I am asked most often is: "How do you get your kids to see you as their teacher when all you have been before is their mother?" and "How do you get your kids to do their schoolwork?" or "Isn't it hard to get them to sit down and do schoolwork when they would rather play?" More often than not, these mothers want to know how to induce their child to decide to do what the mother wants him to do. There is no mention made of obedience . . . Mom doesn't want to be the bad guy.

Before we go any further, it is important that we get straight some basic facts about parents and children. Where do we get these facts? From the Bible. Why do we go to the Bible to find out about parents and children? Because the Bible is the owner's manual for human beings, issued by the Maker in order that we fulfill the purpose for which we were intended and in so doing get the most out of our lives.

If I buy a blender, I can do whatever I want with it. I can read the owner's manual and "use as directed," or I can try to make sand out of rocks with it. It is mine. I bought it. What I do with my blender within the four walls of my house is my business, but if I don't follow the directions, it won't last. I am capable of ruining it to the point that the manufacturer will have to repair it or replace it if it is to ever serve its purpose again.

It is the same with my life. It is my life and I have the freedom to live it and do with it exactly what I choose. If I am smart, I will read the owner's manual God thoughtfully provided— the Bible— and find out how to make it work. I really could be ruining it and not even know it! How wonderful that God gave us this information! How often we live as though there were no way to know how or how not to live our lives. We are so eager to listen to other human beings rather than our Creator.

What Is Not True

First I would like to talk about what is not true about parents and children. There is a very strong humanistic voice in the child-rearing circles of our society. Here is what this voice says:

❑ Children are born into this world totally innocent and sinless. Left to their own inclinations, they will do what is right.

❑ Children are incredibly open, selfless and pure: a blank slate on which the world (and especially the parents) may write.

❑ Children are very fragile. You never know when some seemingly small thing could produce lifelong problems later in life (like a rough birth, not being breast-fed, abrupt or early weaning, or being allowed to cry for longer than five minutes). Parents must be very careful not to upset them.

❑ Children instinctively know what they need, so we must take our cues from them.

❑ Children who are given all that they need (see above), will grow up to be marvelously loving, good and unselfish. This is because they will never have felt unloved due to unmet "needs."

❑ While it is true that a mother must protect her child from danger (this little being is not yet aware that dangers exist in his perfect world), there is some question as to whether one human being has the right to enforce his will upon another. This is especially true since the child is pure and good, and the mother may still be working through problems of her own stemming from the traumas of her own childhood.

This philosophy is pure humanism. It comes from the belief that man is basically good, that he is the end-product of millions of years of evolution and can attain the highest good given the proper environment and encouragement. Humanists teach that a child is born into the world with everything he needs to become whatever he wants to become. If he doesn't achieve his full potential, it is because he wasn't made aware of his potential, was damaged emotionally at some point, or was not given a nurturing environment in which to develop.

This is the child-rearing philosophy that is taught, with varying degrees of emphasis, all over our country (and in other countries as well) by a large organization that was originally formed to help nursing mothers. This way of thinking about parents and children is being swallowed hook, line, and sinker by many Christian women across the country who don't have the discernment to compare what they are hearing with what the Bible teaches. It is very appealing because it seems so gentle and loving, so "pro-motherhood" in a careerist society.

A good steak dinner laced with strychnine is far more dangerous than a clearly marked bottle, especially if you are hungry. The church and the extended family have failed to offer much needed support to new mothers. Older women are to *"train the young women to love their husbands, to love their children . . . that the Word of God may not be dishonored."* The world has stepped in with tainted help.

What Does the Bible Teach?

❑ Children are born into the world with a sinful nature. The Bible teaches that evil comes from within the heart of man rather than from outside influences.

There is nothing outside the man which going into him can defile him; but the things which proceed out of the man are what defile the man . . . For from within, out of the heart of men, proceed the evil thoughts and acts of sexual immorality, thefts, murders, adulteries, deeds of coveting and wickedness, as well as deceit, sensuality, envy, slander, pride and foolishness. All these evil things proceed from within and defile the man. (Mark 7:15, 21-23)

The heart is deceitful above all things, and desperately wicked: who can know it? (Jer. 17:9)

It is hard to see a tiny baby as a sinner, but we know that it is true because the Bible says it is true. Just as adult giraffes give birth to baby giraffes, adult sinners give birth to baby sinners. Our sinfulness is part of our inherent nature. We are not sinners because we sin; we sin because we are sinners.

❑ **Children are foolish and self-centered.** Foolishness is the belief that "I will be happy if I can have what I want." Children do not need to be taught to be selfish and mean, tell lies, take things that they know do not belong to them, hit, kick, bite, and pull hair. They must be taught not to do these things.

Foolishness is bound up in the heart of a child, but the rod of correction will drive it far from him. (Prov. 22:15)

❑ If children are not trained and disciplined, they will become a grief to their parents and a cancer to society.

The rod and reproof give wisdom, but a child who gets his own way brings shame to his mother. (Prov. 29:15)

❑ It is the parents' God-given responsibility to train up their children.

Correct your son, and he will give you comfort; he will also delight your soul. (Prov. 29:17)

Train up a child in the way he should go, even when he is old he will not depart from it. (Prov. 22:6)

And these words, which I am commanding you today, shall be on your hearts; and you shall teach them diligently to your sons and shall talk of them as you sit in your house and when you walk in the way and when you lie down and when you rise up. (Deut. 6:6,7)

❏ It is better to discipline them with a rod than to allow them to grow up to be fools.

Do not hold back discipline from the child, although you beat him with the rod he will not die. You shall beat him with the rod, and deliver his soul from Sheol [an untimely death]. (Prov. 23:13-14)

❏ A child who is not disciplined by his parents will grow up feeling unloved.

My son, do not regard lightly the discipline of the Lord, nor faint when you are reproved by Him; for those whom the Lord loves He disciplines, and He scourges every son whom He receives. It is for discipline that you endure; God deals with you as with sons; for what son is there whom his father does not discipline? But if you are without discipline, of which all have become partakers, then you are illegitimate children and not sons. Furthermore, we had earthly fathers to discipline us, and we respected them; shall we not much rather be subject to the Father of spirits and live? . . . All discipline for the moment seems not to be joyful, but sorrowful; yet to those who have been trained by it, afterwards it yields the peaceful fruit of righteousness. (Heb. 12: 5-11)

What a contrast we see here! The Biblical view is 100 percent opposite to the humanistic view. They cannot both be true, so we must choose which we will believe, and then base all of our child-rearing decisions on that foundation.

At first glance, the first approach seems much nicer—very positive, affirming, nurturing, and "loving." If it is true that children are naturally good and all that, then these methods of child-training would be great. But any philosophy must be built on a basic premise, and if that basic premise is false, the whole system is doomed to failure. We know that the Bible gives us a different premise on which to build our child-training philosophy: children are born sinners. If that is true, then we have our work cut out for us and we don't have to feel guilty when they act like sinners.

My heart really goes out to these ladies who are trying to raise their kids the humanistic way. They try so hard, but their children's very nature is against them. From "nursing on demand" they progress to "life on demand." The world revolves around a child who is not only selfish and foolish, but also smart enough to take advantage of his mother's helpless adoration.

I am all for breastfeeding. I nursed all my babies on demand for the first few months until each child and I found a comfortable schedule. I have had four of my seven babies at home, taught childbirth preparation classes for both home and hospital births, delivered a few babies, helped many breastfeeding mothers and am, in short, very much into mothering. I am not a child hater or an abusive mother.

With all this in mind, I have had a lot of first-hand contact with the mothers and children who are the result of laissez-faire child-raising theories. I can often pick them out on the street, at the park and in stores. The kids tend to be peevish and unhappy, demanding, and unfriendly. The mothers are constantly making excuses for their child's antisocial behavior: "Oh! He hasn't eaten yet." "It's past her nap time." "I haven't given him enough attention this morning." These moms are terribly guilt-ridden. After all, if they were doing it right, their children would not be so bratty; they would be sweet, loving, and friendly.

I have seen these kids scream at their mothers and hit them when they were too slow about "hopping to." I have seen five-year-olds yank at the mother's blouse and demand her breast when they weren't getting enough attention. One mother I know asked me for advice on weaning her almost-two-year-old. It was a little rough since they believed in the "family bed." Six months later I saw her at a park and asked how it had gone. She said she was still working on it; that she had moved her mattress into her daughter's room, but was moving it away from the child's mattress one inch each night, and that she was now two feet from the door. She hoped that in a month or so she could get down the hall to sleep with her husband again. This couple's marriage was never the same after they had this child.

I call these poor ladies choke-chain mothers. They are virtual slaves of their children. Catering to every whim of a child who basically cares nothing for his mother's needs or interests is very draining. At some point, some of these moms really come unglued and scream and yell and hit, or maybe throw things. Then the guilt is horrible! New depths of fawning and groveling are usually the result, and the child knows who has misbehaved.

Often a mother who pursues this approach comes to the point where she feels like a complete failure. In desperation, she finds a good "nurturing" preschool where the child is given the freedom to become his own little person, and she gets a job that makes her feel like she can do something right. The ladies in her nursing support group or play group can't imagine what went wrong. Later, some call her for the name of that great school where her child is enrolled. They discuss how wonderful it is that the child now has a social life, and how much more one has to offer a child when one is not with him all day ("quality time").

Others stick it out until kindergarten, but the diehards may choose to home school. New questions arise. What if the child doesn't like to do math? What if he refuses to do the work? How do you cause a child to want to learn what you want him to learn? A good teacher can motivate her students, right? Maybe the child really knows best and isn't ready . . . If you have more than one or two kids, and they all want to do something different, which one wins? How do you teach some without neglecting the others (a serious problem which could result in emotional trauma). All this doesn't jive with the Magical Child who is sweet, open and eager to learn . . . unfolding like a flower with each new revelation of his beautiful world.

A child who gets his own way brings shame to his mother. (Prov. 29:15)

We must be obedient to the Word of God as we raise our children.

Tell Me How to Begin . . .

If after reading what has been written so far in this chapter, you feel that maybe you have been barking up the wrong tree in your child-rearing approach, it is not too late to change. First, realize that as a believer, you are accountable for what the Word of God says. If you have been following a worldly philosophy in the area of raising your children, you need to confess before God your neglect of His Word and resulting disobedience.

God has probably been trying to speak to you through others also about this area of your life. Has your husband felt that the kids were getting away with a lot? Did your mother make comments to the effect that they are uncontrolled? How about your in-laws, neighbors, and friends? Humbly admit to the Lord that you have been wrong, and ask for His mercy for your children and His special grace for you as you purpose to be obedient.

Child discipline is not merely a technique to get well-behaved children. We parents must obey the Lord, and it is God's Word that tells us to train our children. God does not promise godly children to those who spank. He promises to bless the children of the righteous (obedient). If we are not willing to be obedient to the Lord, it will be difficult to teach our children to obey us.

The reason we are here on earth rather than in heaven is so that we can become godly (Christlike) examples in a perverse world. Most of our non-Christian friends will never see Jesus until they see Jesus in us. It is so important that we be obedient to the Word of God so that we give an accurate picture.

Godliness does not come any more naturally to us than it does to our children. We don't really like to do things God's way. We don't *like* to obey our husbands. It is *hard* to train our children. We don't *want* to forgive. It just isn't *natural* to hold our tongues, or to bless those who curse us, or to do good to those who despitefully use us. That is why Paul says to Timothy, *"For physical training is of some value, but godliness has value for all things, holding the promise for both the present life and the life to come."* Godliness is not easy; that is why we must train ourselves to obey.

Do you want godly children? Is that the desire of your heart? *"Delight yourself in the Lord, and He will give you the desire of your heart."* Are you making sacrifices in order to make sure your kids turn out well? *"To obey is better than sacrifice; and a broken and a contrite heart I will not despise."* Do you really love the Lord? *"If you love me, you will keep my commandments."* Our business is not primarily to make sure our kids come out right. Our primary purpose is to glorify God. We do this by being obedient . . . becoming Christlike. When we are obedient to the Word of God, we can then see the promises of God manifest in our lives. This brings glory to God because people can see that the promises of God are true. Others can see the faithfulness of God in our lives, as well as the peaceful fruits of righteousness, and can glorify (praise and honor) Him.

It may seem difficult at first to turn from a worldly way of looking at child-rearing that appears logical, to what the Bible says, which may appear harsh. It is really a matter of obedience to God. As Christians, if we are to see Him at work in our lives, we must follow Him in every aspect of our lives. The very best thing we can do for our children is be obedient ourselves.

I would suggest that you go to your bookcase and eliminate the books that you have been referring to that don't support what is taught in the Word of God. Next, buy some books that do. Some of our favorites are listed in the "Recommended Reading" section at the end of this book. Talk to other moms you know who you can see are looking to Scripture for direction in training their children. *"Have nothing to do with godless myths and old wives' tales; rather, train yourself to be godly."*

It is important to remember that God gave children parents because they need us! It is our job to teach our children to obey us. This is not based on the fact that we are perfect or even obedient ourselves. It is based on the authority that has been given to us by God over our children. If a policeman stops us for running a red light, we can't say, "You have no right to give me a ticket! You do things wrong yourself, you know! And besides, you have a grumpy attitude!" No, he has a right and a duty to give us a ticket based on the fact that we did wrong and he has been given the authority to stop us when we do wrong. His personal righteousness or personality have nothing to do with it.

What Kids Need

Children need to be taken from parent control, to self-control, to God control. This is the big picture that a parent needs to keep in mind

First, children need to be under their parents' control. Little children do not have self-control and do not naturally do the right thing. We must train them to do right. What do they need to learn? Initially, they need to learn obedience and respect for other people and for property. *"Children, obey your parents in the Lord, for this is right." "Honor your father and mother (which is the first commandment with a promise)." "Love thy neighbor as thyself."* Let's begin with obedience because, once you teach them to obey, they can learn the other things easily.

Obedience involves doing the will of another who has authority in your life. It means doing what you are told to do instead of what you wanted to do. It is our job to make them obey us (parent control) until they learn to choose to obey us (self-control) and then learn to choose to obey the Lord (God control).

An adult who has never learned to obey an authority in his life has a very difficult time learning to obey the Lord. Knowing that obedience to the will of God is what produces real peace and fulfillment, we see how important it is to teach our children to be obedient. It is important to keep in mind the overall goal. It is so easy to let the kids be disobedient because it just doesn't seem worth making an event over some minor thing like staying in the car seat or not jumping on the bed. But if you have made a rule you must enforce it for the sake of your child's walk with the Lord later in life.

I think it is important to be very careful about the rules that you make. Keeping in mind that the child is a sinner, don't tackle everything at once. Figure out the things that are important right now and work on those. You can let some things slide for the time being by not including them in "the law." For example, let's say my four-year-old child is a messy eater, won't stay in his seatbelt, wets the bed, thinks it is funny to run the other way when I call, leaves his clothes on the floor, forgets to empty the trash, and refuses to kiss Aunt Myrtle good-bye, much to my embarrassment. The only ones on that list that I would make an obedience issue out of are staying in the seatbelt and not coming when called. The others can be chalked up to immaturity, childishness and, in the case of Aunt Myrtle, personal dignity.

This is not to say that those other things are not areas that need work, but that these things can be dealt with by verbal instruction, behavior charts and rewards, and by loss of privileges.

Direct disobedience needs to be dealt with firmly. I have found that spanking is very effective in countering disobedience. Spanking is not hitting. I agree that hitting is not good. When an adult gets angry and hauls off and smacks a kid, that adult is teaching the child that a violent response is acceptable. The adult also loses his dignity and the respect of the child. Spanking is not a punishment either. Spanking should be discipline. I tell my kids, "I am going to give you this spanking so that the next time you think about unbuckling your seatbelt and climbing into the back seat you will remember how much your bottom hurt when you did it last time." When a little child pulls on the tablecloth and a vase falls off and bonks him on the head, it works the same way. He is not as likely to pull on the table-cloth again. Pain does teach! But it is important that the spanking be the consequence of the child's disobe-dience, not the fruit of the parents' wrath.

Here are a couple of systems that have been very helpful to me. These are just some suggestions that may help you in your thinking about teaching your chil-dren to obey. The beauty of this approach is that I am as much bound by it as my kids are, so I can't really fly off the handle, nor can I be inconsistent based on my moods. It is all there, posted on the wall in black and white, so that when someone misbehaves he knows what to expect and I know what needs to be done.

The Swat Chart

❏ CAUSING TROUBLE   1 SWAT
Taunting, teasing, badgering, baiting, "start-ing it," etc.

❏ AGGRESSIVE BEHAVIOR   3 SWATS
Hitting, biting, kicking, tripping, slapping, elbowing, scratching, kneeing, or anything done with the intent to hurt.

❏ NAME CALLING   2 SWATS
Calling a person by a name other than his or her own that is not complimentary.

❏ BAD LANGUAGE   10 SWATS
I only had to do this once.

❏ DISRESPECT OR DISOBEDIENCE 5 SWATS
Verbal or nonverbal back talk, not doing what you are told to do.

I use a good long-handled wooden (oak) spoon to serve up the swats, and I reserve the right to do it as hard as I feel is appropriate. My kids do not have to drop their pants, but they do have to bend over the bed by themselves. Swats are not administered in public. The "talking to," swats, and hugs are done behind closed doors to preserve the dignity of the guilty. Sometimes I have to hold court in my bedroom or the downstairs bathroom in order to get all of the facts straight. I either call in the suspects at different times or allow each to speak in turn with no interruptions. If that doesn't give me a clear picture of who did what, I call in witnesses. I am the only one who examines the witnesses. After all is out in the open, I ask each suspect what he did wrong in this situation . . . no excuses! Then based on that, we figure out who gets how many.

For example: Daniel kept opening the bedroom door when David asked him to leave it shut (one swat). When Daniel stuck his head in the door, David slammed it on his head (three swats). Daniel called David a dummy and kicked him (2 + 3 = 5 swats). David called Daniel a brat and pushed him out of the room and made him fall down (five swats). At this point I arrive on the scene . . .

Final Score: Daniel 6, David 8.

Conclusion: Daniel was asking for it, but David should have called me to take care of Daniel rather than resorting to violence.

As our kids have gotten older, we have revised this somewhat. Here is a copy of the house rules. I was trying to include my large age-span family. This chart is also very helpful. Please keep in mind that you will want to customize these to fit your own household and philosophy. I suggest that Mom and Dad sit down and work out the rules together. The key is to make the rules based on general principles so that there aren't too many of them. Picky little rules are agony and can never be consistently enforced.

House Rules

❑ RULE: TREAT EVERYONE KINDLY. This means you don't belittle anyone either to their face or when they aren't there. Don't hurt each other, but rather look out for each other's safety.

CONSEQUENCE: Restriction (loss of privilege) or 3 swats.

❑ RULE: OBEY YOUR MOM AND DAD. This means you do what you are asked to do without complaining or saying,"I'll do it later" or "How come I always . . . " or "How come he never . . . " The parents of a family have every right to ask their children to do anything that would be helpful around the house. They also have a right to say what a child may or may not do.

CONSEQUENCE: Loss of privilege or an added job. If defiance or rebellion is involved, swats will be given.

❑ RULE: ASK PERMISSION: This means that before using or handling something belonging to another person, you must ask. If that person is not available, you don't touch it. This also means that you *ask*, not tell, your parents before you make plans to go somewhere or do something.

CONSEQUENCE: The payment of $1 to the person whose property is involved, or 2 swats. For not asking permission to go, restricted activities.

❑ RULE: DO YOUR CHORES EVERY DAY. This means that each person has jobs to do around the house and each person is expected to do them at first opportunity without being unduly nagged and reminded.

CONSEQUENCE: Since having to be reminded is a sign of irresponsibility, each reminder after the first will cost you 25¢. (The parents will be restricted to one reminder per five-minute period.)

❑ RULE: BE HOME BY . . . This means that you shouldn't leave home without knowing when you should return, and then you should return by that time. The rule will be: Be home by 5:45 P.M. every afternoon, and by 10:00 P.M. each evening (older kids). Exceptions may be made only in advance or in situations completely out of your control.

CONSEQUENCE: For not coming in as arranged, your going out will be restricted.

It is a good idea to put all fines that you charge in a special fund for a special night out or for a missionary project. This way the kids can't accuse you of trying to get rich at their expense.

About Home Schooling . . .

Enough on general principles. Now on to the specifics as to how this applies to teaching your children at home.

First of all, if your children don't obey you, you will have a hard time teaching them. Your first job is to teach them to obey and to respect you and your word. If this is something new for your family, you may need to spend the first semester just working on this. Or maybe you should work on it for a while before you take them out of school.

We had one lady in our school that found out in the first month of home schooling that she had no control over her kids. She had had the older ones in school and had just tuned the little ones out. The oldest girl was pretty obedient but easily discouraged. The younger three were wild, loud and demanding, and then there was a baby. When I would talk to her on the phone, I could hardly hear because of the deafening noise of crying, screaming and shouting in the background. Most of this noise was directed at the mom, but she just tuned it out and went on talking.

She could not even teach them to be quiet on command, let alone teach them math or spelling! After the first semester the older girl was taught by another home school family, and the rest went into public school. The story does not end here! The mom got some counselling, read a lot of books about child training and discipline, and worked on it in the evenings and then all summer. By the next fall, she was ready to try again. Things went much better, and she is still doing it after four years. She is a lot calmer, and her kids are nice and well-behaved and have done well academically. Bravo! I love a success story!

"Because I said so, and I'm the mother!" is a good reason for a child to do his reading assignment. In the classroom you should not put up with any more sassiness, backtalk or disobedience than you do elsewhere in the house. By the same token, if you have not taught your kids to obey in other areas, you cannot expect them to respond to you differently now that you are their teacher as well as their mother.

In your teaching you need to determine what is disobedience and what is just childish fooling around. Do not spank for picky little stuff, and don't reward for normal good behavior. Goodness has its own rewards!

Unpleasant consequences resulting from poor behavior works very well in the classroom. As with swats, figure out in advance what you want done or do not want done. Then decide what will or not happen as a result. For example:

- ❏ Lunch will be served only when assigned work is completed.

- ❏ Student may have a social life on the weekends only if all work for the week is done.

- ❏ Bonus stickers (or pennies) for very neat pages.

- ❏ An ice cream cone is awarded after five books are read.

- ❏ Sloppy work must be redone.

- ❏ Incorrect problems must be reworked until correct.

- ❏ If the assignment is not completed in a given reasonable time frame, more work is required before the whole is considered done.

- ❏ Whining and complaining result in extra assignments.

- ❏ Diligent students earn an extra field trip or park day.

- ❏ Give the child the same number of pennies as the flash cards you will be doing, and he gives you one for each card he misses, the rest he keeps. (This would not be a daily occurrence.)

Some children are naturally more internally motivated than others. These kids will more readily do what they are told and complete their assignments with a minimum of supervision. Others are externally motivated (most of mine fall into this category) and need an axe hanging over their heads in order to get anything done.

If you were the type of student that was internally motivated and you have kids who are externally motivated, you are in for some surprises. You probably thought that all kids learned like you do. You found it easy to believe that kids at home would be highly motivated to start all kinds of learning projects and really run with it. You figured that if you waited long enough they would teach themselves to read and begin tackling the multiplication tables from the sheer joy of learning. But they don't. They see it as work, and boring work at that. When they are "doing school," they are not usually having fun, and that's a drag! They balk at workbooks, flash cards and reading on their own, and reject any games that look educational.

Always remember the following slogan which, as you have not heard it, I shall now recite:

> *School doesn't have to be fun,*
> *It just has to be done!*

If this child needs external motivation, you are there to provide it. You are not a failure if you can't make him love every minute of schoolwork, or love any of it for that matter. Your job is not to win a popularity contest, but rather to teach your kids what they need to know in order to be productive adults. If this home-taught child reaches age thirteen and he still can't read well, multiply or follow directions, you have blown it. The fact that the public schools have that kind of results rather often is no excuse.

I think that too often we home school moms make things too easy for our kids by answering too many questions. We need to make it worthwhile for the kids to think and work. For example, when I taught my nephew one year, he always wanted me to "help" him find the answers in science and social studies. First of all, I informed him that the book never asked a question that was not answered in the book. He didn't believe me, so I showed him all of the answers in one chapter. On the next assignment, he was sure he'd found an exception, so I checked and let him know that the answer was indeed there on page 48. The next time I merely checked, then said, "Yes, it is in the chapter," closed the book and handed it back to him. After that, he didn't figure it was worth asking and found the answers himself.

The same goes for reading directions. Usually when my kids say, "I don't get it!" I have them read the directions aloud to me and show me what it means. (Auditory learners will especially benefit from reading directions aloud, even to themselves.) This way, if there is something they really don't understand I will know what it is. Pretty soon they learn to go through this process on their own. These are lessons in elementary problem-solving that the kids need to learn. If we spoon-feed them too long, they will be handicapped.

Math problems that are done incorrectly should be done aloud by the student for the mom so that they can both see where he got fouled up. When Mom says, This problem is wrong, you should have done it this way," she is missing out on a real teaching opportunity. Have the child explain step by step what he did to get the answer. He will probably catch the mistake as he goes, but if not, you can more easily explain which step he did incorrectly. This process is a pain, and if the child knows this might have to be done with every missed problem he is more likely to be careful in the first place.

Composition skill is another area that can be taught better if Mom does not help too much. For example, instead of actually showing a child the mistakes in a paragraph he has written, say, "There are two spelling mistakes, one punctuation mistake, and one sentence doesn't make sense. Find your mistakes and correct them." When the child has the inconvenience of finding and correcting his own mistakes, he soon finds it easier not to make mistakes to begin with.

We have a home schooling friend who taught in a Vacation Bible School class this summer. About half of the kids in the class were home schooled and half were not. She said that the home-taught kids were much more demanding of her time than the others and seemed to want everything personally explained to them. This is not good. Our kids need to learn to figure things out for themselves. The fact that our kids get more one-on-one attention has its advantages, but we must be careful not to foster laziness and dependency. The idea that adults should drop everything at the whim of the child is just the kind of foolishness that the Bible says we are to discourage.

You are the mother. If you have taken on the responsibility for educating your child, you must educate him. That includes making him do the work that needs to be done. Home teaching means lengthening the list of things you must make your kids do. (When you send your kids to school, you are hiring someone else to do some of the dirty work.) In addition to making them brush their teeth, straighten their room, set the table, be home by 5:00 P.M., you must also make them read aloud, do math problems, write compositions, etc.

The methods you use to accomplish these tasks should be kind, reasonable, and firm. Basically, the techniques for getting children to do what they are not willing to do are the same, whether the issue is household chores or schoolwork. If your child already knows how to obey, it will be much easier for all concerned. If he does not, you have a battle to win first.

Nothing magical takes place in either the child or the mother when one decides to home school. Often family relationships do improve, because in the course of home schooling the children learn to obey. That's not magic . . . that's hard work!

The bottom line is that if these kids are to learn what they need to know (and for the most part they will not learn all they need to know just for the fun of it), they must do what they are told to do. If you can't make them do that, maybe they would be better off in school.

When Not *to Home School*

❏ When your *husband* is not behind it.

❏ When you are not able to make your *children* do what they are told to do.

❏ When *you* are not willing or able to do what needs to be done.

❏ When you and your child are ready for a *different learning situation.* Nowhere in the Bible does it say it is a sin to send your child to school, even public school. However, we must bear in mind that just as the goals of home teachers are not just academic, but first and foremost moral and spiritual, the public schools are in the business of molding little minds into the thinking of humanism, feminism, globalism, and now New Age-ism. Think twice, then again, before sending your child into the hands of a program that censors God out and leaves all this in.

❏ When the child reaches the point where *you can no longer meet his academic needs,* either because of your educational background, his learning problems, or because teaching your younger children takes all of your time and energy and the older one is not self-motivated.

Check out all of the options. We know moms who have worked out trades. People who hire tutors are happy with their tutoring arrangements. In our area we also have a "cottage school" that has sprung out of home schooling. One woman teaches about fourteen kids in her home several hours a day. The younger kids come in the morning and the older ones in the afternoon. She does the main teaching and the moms help with assignments. The parents teach subjects such as Bible and history.

We have yet another option in our area called "Alternative Christian High School." This is a small, limited-enrollment, year-round program where the kids learn at their own pace but have a lot of help and supervision from the teacher. The families who have used it have been pleased.

Grandparents have also risen to the challenge of teaching their grandkids, as have aunties, and older sisters (aged twenty and up), and daughters-in-law. You see, you aren't stuck with a choice between total home schooling with you as the one and only teacher, and Public School Number 42 down the block. Leave no stone unturned!

13

Plain Talk About Teaching Other People's Kids

"This is working so well, why not offer to teach the whole neighborhood?"
— Ima Nutt, home teaching mother

fter you have been successfully home teaching for a while, friends, relatives, and neighbors will notice the good results. In the face of this approval, you are apt to offer to help someone out of a bad situation by teaching their child. You think, "After all, I am already in the routine. One more won't make that much difference. A situation with less pressure and more discipline is exactly what this child needs, and my children do get along well with him." *Think again!* This is not a matter to enter into lightly. We recommend *much* prayerful consideration before ever making such an offer.

There is no question that this is an opportunity for loving service. You can, and probably will, be a help to the child academically, emotionally, even spiritually. Most likely, the parents will even pay you, and that will ease the tight financial situation most families with stay-at-home mothers find themselves in. It is very tempting.

However, the addition of an outsider, even a beloved outsider, to your home school often brings many problems that do not become obvious until the deed is done. The situation is entirely different from a family-only home school and entirely different from a conventional school.

We speak from experience. The authors have both taught other children in our homes and have talked with other women who have done so. The situations had so much in common that we feel there are some definite, consistent drawbacks to teaching other people's kids.

The most likely candidates that will be attracted to school in a home other than their own seem to fall into four general categories:

❑ The Lost Sheep

❑ One of the Family

❑ The Exception

❑ The Trade

We will consider each situation separately, because although all four have much in common, each also brings its own unique problems and considerations.

We will not be addressing the one-room schoolhouse. In this situation, a mom has more than one or two kids who come each day whose parents consider her home school a private school and pay tuition accordingly.

The Lost Sheep

This is usually a child who has been in school and is miserable. He is probably doing poorly academically. He may be disliked, ridiculed, or shunned by his classmates or he may be inclined to hang around with the bad kids. Often his parents have tried everything they can think of within their financial means: public school, private school, special education, tutoring, counseling. Nothing seems to help. Home schooling seems to be made-to-order for this child.

Please keep in mind that the troubles he is having are likely caused largely by his own bad habits, strangeness, lack of self-discipline, or lack of motivation. The fact that other children did not like him may have been because he wasn't very likable, or his choice of friends may reflect deep anger towards authority. Maybe he bragged, gloated, and lied, or was unkind, rude, and defiant. In the difficult school situation he has been facing, the school was not the only problem. He was probably a big part of the problem.

His mother may also have been a big part of the problem, concerned though she may be. You may notice when you talk with the mother that she tends to blame all of the child's problems on all of the schools and teachers where he has been. But if you were to check with these sources, you might find that in their opinion, much of what they had tried to accomplish was sabotaged by the mother. Perhaps she shielded him from situations that caused any unpleasantness by writing notes when he wasn't sick, not making him do his homework, and making excuses for him. In so doing she may have rescued him from the consequences of his own sinful, foolish, or irresponsible actions.

You will be dealing with this same child and this same mother. Changing the circumstances is not going to change the people involved. If she did not allow the previous school to discipline him, will she let you? Once he leaves your home, will his mother reinforce what you have said to him or will she undermine you?

You are not the final authority in this child's life. If he doesn't finish his schoolwork in the time you have allotted for it, will you be able to do anything about it? Have his parents seen to it that he got his home assignments done in the past?

Because this child is extremely needy, he is going to require a lot more from you than your own comparatively normal children. Providing for his needs will likely consume your thoughts, time, and emotions with very little left for your own kids. You will be giving so much to him and possibly seeing little apparent gain. It can be very frustrating, and it is easy to become angry and resentful towards him and his mother.

The relationship you will have with him will be an extremely intense one, much more like mother and child than teacher and pupil. But the problem is that you are not his mother and he is not your child. In all fairness, while he is in your home you should treat him like you do your own children. But the frustrating thing is that he gets the all good stuff (field trips, cooking projects, math games, individual attention, stories, etc.) without the same accountability. You can make your kids behave. You can restrict their activities, spank them, holler at them, or whatever you think is necessary to get the kind of behavior you want, but this kid goes home at 2:00 P.M.

Another problem arises from the assumptions you make about him. You expect him to be basically like children you are used to—i.e., your own. The fact that you have not raised him from a baby is going to make him different. He has a different upbringing than your children do. Your children's temperament and bent toward specific sins, their abilities and lack of abilities are familiar to you. You understand them. With a child from another family, you don't have this insight into what makes him tick.

The child may also have academic problems that you do not understand because you have never faced them in your own children. If you have not been a classroom teacher you may not have dealt with a wide variety of learning difficulties. For example, maybe after your children learned to sound out words they just naturally understood the stories they read. Now you are trying to help a child that can read every word in a story and still does not understand what is going on.

His home environment is also different from these other children that you know and love. Maybe he eats more sugar and other refined foods than you think is appropriate. He may spend a lot more time in front of a television than your children. He may not have a schedule and bedtime of which you approve and as a result may arrive each morning groggy and lethargic, or he may be higher than a kite from a Sugar Crunch breakfast. All of these areas strongly affect his learning, and you have absolutely no control over them.

What else? Well, since you asked, there is also the problem of how this child gets along with your children. They may have enjoyed playing together every afternoon for the past six months, but how will they do with him as a part-time member of the family? When conflicts arise, it is difficult for the mother to be objective and fair, especially if she is already fed up with the intruder.

Let me give you some examples. In a couple of situations with which we are familiar, the extra child being taught was an only child and did not know how to get along with siblings. He became completely bent out of shape over what was normal sibling behavior, such as pestering, chasing, and playful teasing. In this case, who does the mother correct? Her children, she feels, are acting in a fairly normal way and are not doing anything really wrong. They *do* need to learn to be kind and considerate of other people's feelings, but she is irritated with this kid who seems to be getting upset and making a scene over a very little thing. Since she can't let the kid really have it, the mom often ends up overreacting, usually towards her own kids.

In another situation, we have a child who is used to younger brothers and sisters. He spends his time bossing your children around all day. He has appointed himself policeman and insists on enforcing all of your rules. While the rules do need to be obeyed, you find yourself angrier at this outsider than at the ones who are breaking the rules. It seems like he is trying to make your kids look bad in order to make himself look better. Or he may be in the habit of being mean to the little ones. We're not talking about math and reading anymore, we're talking about child-rearing. You can figure that these types of things will happen every single day. This gets old mighty fast.

Well, considering the fact that "tribulation worketh patience," so far this seems to offer an excellent patience development program for the mother. But how will it affect your kids? Sometimes you will feel that not only is this child messing up the home life of your children but also their academic progress. You will feel responsible to his mother to solve his problems or get him caught up. If you are being paid, there is a tremendous amount of guilt if you don't succeed.

You will often find that you must put a lot more effort into this child than your own. He may end up getting a better education than they do. If he doesn't know how to follow directions and figure things out, you will be explaining things to him all the time. Often a child of this type is very manipulative and has learned very well how to get the lion's share of an adult's attention. He has mastered the *mope*, the *panic*, the *despair*, the *urgent*, and the *poor pitiful pearl*. Your experience probably doesn't cover this caliber of advanced acting. All of the one-on-one attention he receives is time that is not available for your own children.

Teaching this child may be a good thing for *him*, but is it a good thing for *you* and *your children*? I realize that we want to be caring, giving people, and that we want our children to learn to be the same, but are we giving up too much in order to do it? It is not wise to take on something good, and in so doing, give up something better.

One of the Family

This child is a relative who has come to live with you for some reason or another, most likely because of problems at home. He may be a *lost sheep* as well, and if so, most of the previous section applies to him.

You have a couple of advantages in this situation. The fact that this child is a relative means that at least you know the family well. The fact that he is living with you means that you can monitor his home life and all of the associated variables. You can provide consistent discipline and see to it that he is held accountable for his behavior.

The fact that he is living with you also brings a whole new set of problems. You are accountable not only for his academics, but also for his character development. What will you do if he is a compulsive liar? How will you handle it if you find out he is corrupting your children when you are not looking?

One lady we know had a ten-year-old stepson who came to live with them. He would constantly hurt the baby when her back was turned and then deny he did it. It was very difficult to catch him in the act. He was a ward of the state and when they tried to correct him, he would call his social worker and report the parents for child abuse. If the child in question is already involved with Social Services, think twice . . . it could be a problem.

The child you are taking on may be out of his own home because he has become impossible. By God's grace, you may be able to teach him to behave appropriately, but it will require a great deal of patience and persistence. The intensity of the situation is compounded by the urgency of straightening him out before he goes to the dogs, goes home, or becomes a bad influence on your own children. It will be added pressure if you are the only Christian family in your extended family and everyone is watching to see how you will handle the family's "problem." You may feel that the reputation of Christianity is at stake.

If this child is older than your oldest child, you will not always know whether his problems are due to his age or other factors, because of your own lack of experience. He will compete for the position of the firstborn in your family, which is hard on your own firstborn.

Then of course, when you get tired of him, you can't take comfort in the fact that he goes home at

2:00 P.M., or that this is Friday. There is no let-up. There is no let-up for your kids either.

The Exception

I realize that we have painted a pretty bleak picture up to this point. The reason for this is that in most of the situations that we know of, it hasn't worked out very well. There are exceptions, however. Here are some factors that seem to make teaching other people's children work when it does work:

❑ Both mothers agree in their philosophy of child-rearing, and there is mutual trust. The mother *not* teaching is faithful to follow through on assignments and discipline as needed.

❑ The child being taught is the same age or grade level as one of the teacher's children so that she doesn't have to prepare for an extra grade level. There are no learning problems.

❑ It is a big help if the child is already well known to the teacher and respects her and is not a behavior problem.

❑ A fair agreement must be reached about compensation for teaching services. This could be money or services such as dressmaking, housecleaning, baby-sitting, haircutting, or whatever. This only works well if each is faithful to follow through with their part of the agreement and if the agreement is very specific. For example: one dress per month, or all the family's haircuts until June, or $100.00 per month, due on the first, or five hours of housecleaning every Saturday, or whatever.

Remember that if you know that someone's child is going to show up on your doorstep every morning at

8:30 A.M. you'd better be ready. You can't oversleep. It takes some of the spontaneity out of your school schedule. You can't really call off school one day at the last minute and clean house if necessary. If you or your kids are sick, it cuts into the other child's schooltime if you call off classes. This is especially true if the child's mother is at work. Who will watch him if you are sick? You can't usually have an open-ended field trip if the other child has piano lessons at 2:30 P.M. You may also find that it puts the crimp on off-season family vacations and visits from out-of-town relatives.

As you may have noticed, these problems are not insurmountable. Even so, you will be glad every Friday, and count the days until vacation more than the rest of us who are just teaching our own. It is definitely more stressful.

The Trade

In this situation, you offer to trade children with another mother for the course of the school day. Maybe she takes all of the preschoolers and you teach the school-age children. Or maybe you each teach your own kids three days a week, then she takes all of them one day, and you take all of them one day, thus giving each other a day off. Another possibility is that you teach all of the children the subjects that you teach best, and she teaches them all the subjects she teaches best.

These trades often work out very well, but here are a few cautions.

First of all, the mothers involved in the trade need to have very similar, if not identical, values as far as child discipline and educational approach. We recommend that you be sure that there is agreement on basic Christian doctrine, nutrition, and TV philosophy. If these things are not taken into consideration, you can ruin a perfectly good friendship due to misunderstandings. We have known it to happen.

Guidelines

If in spite of all our good advice and solemn warnings you insist on teaching someone else's child, especially in the first two categories, here are some guidelines to follow.

❑ If being paid for your services is appropriate, be sure you are being paid enough to make it worth all the trouble. On bad days it helps to remember, "Well, at least I'm getting paid for this!" Be sure the child is not in your home just because it's such a great bargain for the parents. Don't be the cheapest option. Private tutors charge $10-plus per hour. Private schools charge $120 to $300 per month. Public schools get close to $4,000 per year per child of our tax money. People don't appreciate what they don't pay for (sad, but true).

❑ Commit yourself for only a limited period of time, maybe one semester. Set a time for an *honest* review with the parents after this time period. Discuss how it has been going and only continue if *everyone* (especially you) is happy with the situation. Do this at regular intervals, and *never get yourself into a situation that you can't get out of.*

❑ Don't let this child consume you. For one mom, things became so intense that she lost her temper and was unkind to the child. This shocked her into realizing how sinful and bitter her attitude toward him had become, and she was finally able to repent and put the situation into a proper balance.

Step back and realize how limited you are in what you can accomplish. Do what you can for this child, and don't shortchange your own children. Don't waste effort on things you can do nothing about, such as diet, schedule, homework assignments, general weirdness, and his parents' problems. Love him, encourage him, help him with his math, help him with his reading, pray for him, and be realistic about what you can and cannot do. You can't make a silk purse out of a sow's ear in two semesters.

Remember, God has given you your own children to train. They are your first priority. Please do not make a hasty decision to teach someone else's child in your family school. Sometimes it works, but often it is much less than you'd hoped for. If you find yourself in a situation where you have another child in your home and it is not working out, get out of it as soon as you can. Scripture gives us the guidelines for these types of situations:

> *If you have been snared with the words of your mouth, have been caught with the words of your mouth, do this then, my son, and deliver yourself; since you have come into the hand of your neighbor, go, humble yourself, and importune your neighbor. Do not give sleep to your eyes, nor slumber to your eyelids; deliver yourself like a gazelle from the hunter's hand, and like a bird from the hand of the fowler.*

14

But, Lord!
I Home Schooled
Him!

*"The proof of the pudding
is in the eating."*
— Traditional saying

L et's talk about the nitty-gritty reasons we have chosen to teach our kids at home. I think that for many of us the main reason we home school is to make sure our kids come out all right. Maybe if we teach them the Bible all the time and keep them away from sinful influences they won't be likely to grow up to be a shame to us. How sad and embarrassing it must be for parents whose kids turn out bad!

We must be very careful at this point. While it is good to *desire* that our children follow the Lord, it is asking for trouble to make it our *goal*. Let's talk about the difference between these.

What happens to us and our children if we make it our goal that they come out right? First, a goal is something we can achieve with careful planning and followthrough. We know the goal: a fine, upstanding adult who loves God and of whom we can be proud. But there are so many pitfalls . . . Think about the dangers! Peer pressure, perverts, secular textbooks, values clarification, TV, pornography, rock music, bad movies . . . Home schooling seems to be the best plan to achieve our goal. What better way to control our kids and their environment so they *can't* go wrong!

Is there anything wrong with this reasoning? Yes. Any time you set a *goal* that requires another individual's efforts, cooperation, participation, or enthusiasm, you are setting yourself up for problems. You cannot control other people. Even your own children will ultimately make their own choices. Furthermore, if your goal is that your child turn out a certain way, and he looks like he's not cooperating, you will experience feelings of anger, depression, or anxiety. Your child has the power to thwart the goal which you have so carefully planned to achieve.

You can only control *your own* actions, thoughts, attitudes and words. There is nothing wrong with making reasonable *personal* goals . . . but it is important to remember the difference between personal goals and goals that involve other people's choices.

How then do we look at our responsibility before God to raise godly children? First of all, it is important to make the result of godly children our *desire* rather than our *goal.* Then we must go to God's Word to find out how *He* says we are to raise our children. Our goal should be to obey God's Word. Our own obedience to God is an obtainable goal; our children's obedience is not. They are free moral agents and will stand or fall before God alone, just as we will.

God promises righteous children to the righteous. The emphasis is then on *our* righteousness, not on our children's. What does it mean to be righteous? Will I be righteous if I attend church weekly? Add Wednesday night prayer meeting? Have family devotions? Tithe? Exercise the gifts of the Spirit? Never smoke, drink, or buy lottery tickets? Give sacrificially to missions? Pass out tracts? What could be more righteous than home teaching my kids?

Often we look at the people around us to see what things we need to do to be righteous. In our culture we are satisfied to match or do a little better than those around us. God compares us to Himself, not to other sinners. God does not look on the outward appearance, but on the heart. Being righteous is not what things you do or don't do, but rather what you are as compared to Christ.

The false approach to righteousness keeps us looking at each other rather than to God and His Word. It breeds pride and an attitude of spiritual one-upmanship. When we are feeling proud of ourselves, our self-righteousness keeps us from seeing areas in our lives that need change. We settle for less than conformity to the image of Christ.

It is so easy to do a good thing and then judge everyone who doesn't. We need to put away our spiritual yardsticks and begin comparing ourselves by God's standards rather than man's. This is painful but profitable.

In our current Christian culture we tend to look to men rather than God for our instruction in righteousness. We read books, watch TV, listen to the radio and tapes, and listen to sermons. Even when we go to Bible studies, we tend to pay more attention to what the teacher says than what the Word says. We put a lot of stock in appearances, and we rationalize sins that don't show. What do we read? What movies and TV shows do we watch when the kids are in bed? What do we talk about? What is our motivation? Do we always tell the truth?

We must go to the Word with a mind to obey. Are we really willing to go against the tide . . . even the "Christian" tide? *Sanctified* means set apart for a holy purpose. In this day and age it may mean being set apart from popular Christian culture. We stand or fall before God alone. We alone are responsible for the extent to which we seek God's face and do His will.

God has given us His Word. *"Be not conformed to this world, but be transformed by the renewing of your mind."* We are told that God's Word *"is profitable for* doctrine, for reproof, for correction and for instruction in righteousness, that the man of God may be equipped for every good work." We are instructed to "be doers of the Word and not hearers only." Our righteous deeds are to be the reflection of what we are, the result of a mind transformed by the Word and a heart that looks to Christ as the standard.

What I am trying to say is that home schooling does not guarantee that your child will turn out well. The outcome of your children does not depend on what you *do*, but rather on what you *are*. "Delight yourself in the Lord, and He will give you the desires of your heart." Do you desire godly children? Delight yourself in the Lord!

Some fine Christian young people have come out of the public school system, and there will probably be home-taught children who bring disgrace to the name of Christ. Many a pastor or church family has had children who reject the Lord. Only God knows those who truly desire to be obedient to Him. "Man looks on the outward appearance, but the Lord looks on the heart." We are not to judge each other; God is the righteous Judge. We are to humble ourselves before a holy God. We answer to Him alone for our obedience.

This doesn't mean that we should throw up our hands in despair and turn our children loose into any and every educational and social situation, since "we can't guarantee how they will turn out no matter what we do." Performed with the right spirit and for the right reasons, home schooling *can* make a difference. We have to do our very best, and *then* let God do the rest.

As parents, it is our sober responsibility to be obedient to the Word of God, and to rest in Him with regard to our children. We can't make them obey God—but we *can* demonstrate to them the joy of living in humble obedience to a loving Father. We *can* protect them from known evil influences and give them a taste of spiritual honey. We *can* discipline their habits and guide their thinking.

God will one day call us to account and ask us if we have done these things. We must be obedient to the Word in the areas of parenting and child-training as much for our own sakes as for the sakes of our children.

When the time comes for our children to make their own choices, we can pray for them and continue to be godly examples. But we must understand that we have all learned some things the hard way and that our kids are no exception. If we are striving to walk in obedience to the Lord, we can let our children go when the time comes and trust God to work in their lives as He has worked in ours.

As I write this, I am convicted of my own disobedience to the Lord. I pray that the Lord will, in His grace, spare my children from the consequences of my shortcomings. I am no more perfect than you are. I struggle with impatience and irritation. I am not always kind. I am selfish and undisciplined in my use of time. But I *want* to be like Him! And I know that He cares more for them than I do and is able to protect and guide them.

Lord, free us from external standards that allow us to settle for less. Give us the courage to come to Your Word with hearts willing to change. Don't let us be comfortable with "good enough." Let us hear Your voice above all the other voices that would tell us things are okay when they are not. May we keep our eyes on You. Lord, bring every thought into captivity. Transform us by the renewing of our minds. Help us not to worry about anything, but rather tell You every detail of our needs in earnest and thankful prayer, that the peace of God may keep constant watch over our hearts and minds in Christ Jesus. May our lives demonstrate Your transforming power and bring glory to Your holy name. Amen.

15

Serving Other Home Schoolers

He comforts us in all our
affliction so that we may be
able to comfort those
who are in any affliction . . .
— 2 Corinthians 1:4

When I decided to home teach my children six years ago, I was the only one I knew who was even thinking of it. I had read an interview with secular home school leader John Holt in a magazine. The whole idea was new to me and opened up all sorts of possibilities I had never considered. I thought about it for a whole year before I took the plunge. Everyone thought I was very strange. Just when I had four out of six kids in school and could breathe a little, I was taking them all out! However, people were somewhat used to my doing things differently. Not only did I have six (and a half, at the time) kids, but three of them had been born at home, and there seemed to be no end to the outlandish things I would try.

Somewhere I came across a flyer for a four-day retreat with Raymond Moore. This was the first I had heard of the man and I knew nothing of his books. Off we went to the retreat and had a wonderful time. We came back all enthused and with the address of a school that would send us curriculum. After testing the boys and sending in all the necessary paperwork, we waited for the books. It was a great day when they arrived! I was sick in bed with pneumonia, eight months pregnant, and trying to run herd on six kids who weren't in school.

I desperately needed a support group, but there wasn't one. In fact, it wasn't long until people were calling *me* and asking questions. Because I was "doing it," I was the local expert. Talk about the blind leading the blind! I had decided to make my motto for the first year *muddle through* and I was doing just that. I consoled myself with the thought that I *couldn't* do worse than some public schools, and thus I survived.

At that time, the best way to home teach in California and comply with the law was for each family to file an affidavit and become its own private school. In our county, the local authorities didn't buy this idea. They contacted many of the schools listing one teacher and only a few students. Somehow I ended up being the only one in our area who wasn't contacted by the school district. When people called and asked if they should file an affidavit, I didn't know what to tell them.

One day I had a bright idea: If these families enrolled their kids in our "private school," they could home teach their children, comply with the compulsory attendance law, and still not call undue attention to themselves. One of my home schooling friends was a state-credentialed teacher. I called to see if she would like to run a school with me. She said yes, so we took the kids to the beach and while they played we founded Painter Avenue Christian School.

We decided that if we were going to do this, we needed to do everything within our power to be above reproach. We checked out all the laws, looked at what other private schools required, and forged ahead. The fact that these kids would be a part of *our* school made us in some part responsible for their education. Therefore, we had to provide some form of accountability for the parents. My big concern, however, was that we not have so much paperwork for the poor mothers that it would interfere with teaching their children. We kept it to a minimum. A description of goals and curriculum at the beginning of the year, three progress reports during the year, and one teachers' meeting per month were all we required. We charged a minimal tuition to pay for printing, postage, business license, etc.

We started with ten families and had a wonderful time and became good friends. We found out that teachers' meetings during park days don't work well. The kids were all over the park, so the moms were either with the other ladies and unaware of what their kids were doing, or watching their kids and not in on the meeting. It was also difficult to discuss *anything* shouting over the din of the usual park noise. The following year we had the teachers' meetings in the evenings so the kids could stay home with the daddies or sitters. The rest of us got a lot more accomplished. Being with the other moms without the distraction of the children created a better atmosphere for sharing.

Our teachers' meetings are not boring business meetings. Although we do take care of business (like turning in forms, planning outings, and deciding what color the T-shirts will be), the primary purpose is to encourage each other. Often we begin the sharing time with a discussion topic such as, "The thing that makes it all worthwhile is . . . " or "The hardest thing about home teaching is . . . " to get the ball rolling.

It is my experience that what home schooling moms need is *people* rather than more activities. The activities are the icing on the cake, but we can live without them. Sometimes we may even need to go on an "activity diet" if we are involved in too many things. It is counterproductive to have to figure out how to fit school in around the field trips.

Home schooling moms need to get together to bear one another's burdens. Where else can we talk about how it really is? Our neighbors are watching us like hawks, our relatives are sure we have bitten off more than we can chew, and often our husbands have given us one year to prove ourselves. If we complain or let them know we are discouraged, they will often nod and say, "That's what I thought would happen," or, "Don't complain to me. This was your idea. If you don't like it, put them in school!" That is not what we need to hear. Even those friends and family members who are very supportive but are not doing it themselves can't really scratch where it itches when we have problems and doubts.

As we share our problems and frustrations, we find out that we are not alone in our feelings or the problems we face. We also learn that others have found solutions to these very problems. We can laugh together, share common complaints, sympathize and cheer each other up. In a teachers' meeting, we give each other support.

Two are better than one because they have a good return for their labor. For if either of them falls, the one will lift up his companion. But woe to the one who falls when there is not another to lift him up . . . And if one can overpower him who is alone, two can resist him. A cord of three strands is not quickly torn apart.

It is well worth your while to find a home school support group. There are many different types. Some loosely-woven groups consist mainly of casual meetings in a park. You can sometimes find a satellite program associated with an established private school. Independent study programs with associated support groups are yet another variation on the theme.

If you don't know of a support group in your area, organize your own if you feel the Lord is leading you in this direction. The main thing is to get together with other home schoolers on a regular basis. It is so good to talk, compare notes, get ideas, find out you're normal, and get your kids together! If you haven't found any others, keep looking . . . this is a growing movement and there are bound to be more.

I never intended to start a large home school school, but we have grown to nearly 150 families. Now our school is divided into fifteen support groups, according to neighborhoods. We meet with the group leaders once a month, and they have monthly meetings with their groups in their homes. These are the guidelines our leaders use in running the groups.

❏ The purpose of the group is to support (hold up) and encourage (give courage) to each other. Keep this in mind as you guide the discussion. Be a learner yourself, and don't be afraid to share your own problems and frustrations. This will help people realize that they aren't the only ones that face problems. If they see that you aren't ashamed to share, they won't be either.

❏ Be sensitive to differences among your group members. Be especially aware of areas such as church background, approaches to child discipline, views of the gifts of the Spirit, marital status, working mothers (some may have to go back to work later), and any other topic that might be hot. Your position needs to be "godly neutral." By this I mean that we do not compromise the light that the Lord has given us through His Word. We continue to work toward conformity to the image of Christ in our own lives and in our relationships to others, but at the same time allow the Lord to work in the lives of others in different ways and at a different pace.

Accepting others who perhaps see things differently at this point in their walk with the Lord is not compromise. I believe it is the way that God accepts us. You will need to set the example for your group and may even need to speak to some aside, explaining the importance of this kind of unity.

❑ Keep in touch with your people. Some of your new teachers would never have considered home teaching without some kind of support system. We need to be sure that they get what they need to get over the hump. Some will need very little help, some will need extra help just at the beginning, and some will require help throughout the first year.

Call each support group member at least once a month and *plan on talking for a while.* Ask how they are doing. Remember what they say. It means so much to people if you remember their kids' names and ages, what books they are using, when the baby is due, the name of their dog, and that their Grandma is in the hospital. If needed, keep a card file by the phone and take notes to refer to in the future.

Additional note: We have made a point of having almost all information passed along by the group leaders by phone rather than in a newsletter. This gives the leaders a reason to keep in touch with each family in their group. Often people will want to talk but will hesitate to call.

A few feel so poorly about themselves that the normal difficulties of being both mother and teacher convince them that they really are, just as they suspected, utter failures. They may not seek help for fear that the terrible truth will be known. You must be the initiator with these dear people. You will probably need to continue to be the one to call because they can't imagine that you would want to hear from them. Love them like Jesus does, affirm the best in them . . . You may be the best friend they've ever had.

❏ Begin and end each meeting with prayer. This is a ministry the Lord has given you. In a certain sense, you are the shepherd to a small flock. This responsibility should make you humble and careful. *"Let not many of you become teachers, my brethren, knowing that as such we shall incur a stricter judgment."*

❏ It is important to see yourself as a servant of Christ. As a servant of Christ in a leadership role, we serve *Him* by serving others. It can get old if we see ourselves at everybody's beck and call. Being a group leader will involve interruptions, inconvenience, dealings with difficult and inconsiderate people, and a lot of added hassle. If we are serving the Lord, however, rather than people, we can find joy in our service to others.

❏ Never delegate to anyone a job you have not done yourself. Don't ask people to plan field trips, make phone calls, or clean up after a meeting if you haven't done it or aren't willing to do it first. There may come a time when you don't have to do everything, but always be willing. No job should be beneath you.

❏ Don't try to do everything by yourself. Share the joy of serving with others. If you want someone to help you with your work, teach by example. Do the job while they watch, then have them do the job while *you* watch, then let them take it over. *Don't insist that everything be done exactly your way.*

Praise and appreciation are absolutely essential if you want people to keep on helping you. Get specific about what they did that helped, or was a blessing to you, or encouraged others. Keep your eyes open and *notice* what people are doing right.

If you belong to a home school group, please offer to help your leaders. They are usually just moms like you and can't do everything. It is easy for them to spend too much time meeting the needs of others and neglect their own families. You may be able to make phone calls, do filing, watch their children occasionally, etc. Ask what you can do! Make it possible for them to have enough time to teach their own children.

After you offer to help, be reliable. Don't make it easier for your leader to do it herself. Get the information straight, make sure you know what she wants done, and ask questions if you aren't sure. Be prompt about following through. Do the task well so that she won't need to redo it herself, ask you to redo it, or be embarrassed by the final result. What a blessing it is to be able to give a job to someone and forget about it!

Many of us find ourselves reluctant leaders. Somehow we ended up at the front of the parade. While we muddle along by trial and error, others walk confidently in our steps. We must put our trust in the Lord to direct us all. We must not "put our confidence in horses and chariots," but in God.

Except the Lord builds the house, they labor in vain that build it. Except the Lord guard the city, the watchman keeps awake in vain.

So many times we have made plans, but the Lord has stepped in and saved us from mistakes. It seems that every time things have fallen through, the Lord had a better plan.

If you do become the leader of a group of home schoolers, be prepared to learn to be like Jesus. Do a study in the Gospels, paying special attention to how He was treated. Jesus was misjudged, unappreciated, misunderstood, and, in general, not well treated by many of those whom he served. Although this will not be the case most of the time, and there will be many who love you and think you are great, it is important to realize that in serving the Lord in a position of leadership, you *will* receive criticism. Some will assume the worst about your motives. We must try in every way to be above reproach, looking to God rather than man for our approval.

Obedience, perseverance, prayer, and dependence on God are what bring blessing in leadership. Though it's great to be creative or have organizational skills, overdependence on these can bring a snare. Becoming a leader because it feels good to have some power, glory, or money will only bring hurt to yourself and others.

> *Do nothing from selfishness or empty conceit, but with humility of mind let each of you regard one another as more important than himself; do not merely look out for your personal interests, but also for the interests of others.*

As in every other area of our lives, we need to be obedient to God. We need to become more like Jesus whether we are leaders or followers. Then we can hope that our loved, prayed-for, home schooled children will follow where we lead!

RECOMMENDED READING

Ballmann, Ray. *The How and Why of Home Schooling.* Westchester, IL: Crossway Books, 1987.

Blumenfeld, Samuel. *How to Tutor.* Milford, MI: Mott Media, 1973.

Campbell, Ross. *How to Really Love Your Child.* Wheaton, IL: Victor Books, 1977. *

———. *How to Really Love Your Teenager.* Wheaton, IL: Victor Books, 1981.

Collins, Marva and Tamarkin, Civia. *Marva Collins' Way.* Los Angeles: Jeremy P. Tarcher, Inc., 1982.

Dobson, James. *Dare to Discipline.* Wheaton, IL: Tyndale House Publishers, 1973. *

———. *Hide or Seek.* Old Tappan NJ: Fleming H. Revell, 1979.

———. *The Strong-willed Child.* Wheaton, IL: Tyndale House, 1978.

Holt, John. *Teach Your Own.* Boston, MA: Holt Associates, 1981.

Hunt, Gladys. *Honey for a Child's Heart.* Grand Rapids, MI: Zondervan Publishing House, 1979. *

Macaulay, Susan Schaffer. *For the Children's Sake.* Westchester, IL: Crossway Books, 1984. *

——. *How to be Your Own Selfish Pig.* Elgin, IL: David C. Cook Publishing Co., 1982.

McCullough, Bonnie Runyan. *401 Ways to Get Your Kids to Work at Home.* New York: St. Martin's Press, 1981.

Moore, Raymond. *Home Grown Kids.* Waco, TX: Word Books, 1981.

Pride, Mary. *The NEW Big Book of Home Learning.* Westchester, IL: Crossway Books, 1988. *

——. *The Next Book of Home Learning.* Westchester, IL: Crossway Books, 1987.

——. *Schoolproof.* Westchester, IL: Crossway Books, 1988.

——. *The Way Home.* Westchester, IL: Crossway Books, 1985.

Smalley, Gary. *The Keys to Your Child's Heart.* Waco, TX: Word, Inc. *

Trelease, Jim. *The Read Aloud Handbook.* New York: Viking Penguin, 1982.

Wilson, Elizabeth Laraway. *Books Children Love.* Westchester, IL: Crossway Books, 1987.

Winn, Marie. *The Plug-in Drug.* New York: Viking Press, 1977. *

*   We suggest you read these first.

MEET THE
AUTHORS

Luanne Shackelford, the major author, is the mother of seven children, ranging in age from four to sixteen. She has been home teaching her children for the last six years. In addition, Luanne was the founder and director of Painter Avenue Christian School, a private school made up of home schooling families. The school has grown from ten to 140 families in the last five years. Luanne has a reputation throughout Southern California as a pioneer and leader in the local Christian home schooling community. She has counseled and encouraged hundreds of home schooling moms in her living room and over the phone, and has addressed many home school groups. With her family, she is now serving as a missionary under the ministry of International Missions, Inc. in Mindanao in the Philippines.

Susan White, the primary author of the chapters on testing, scheduling, and teaching other people's children, is the mother of two totally home schooled daughters, ages nine and seven. Before Susan's children were born, she taught in the public school system for five years. Susan has been working with other home schoolers for the past three years. She is presently a support group leader and the assistant director of Painter Avenue Christian School. Susan lives with her husband Michael and daughters Renada and Michaela in Whittier, California.